Business
Minded

Business Minded

A GUIDE TO SETTING UP YOUR MIND, BODY, AND BUSINESS FOR SUCCESS

CARLY A. RIORDAN

Publisher Mike Sanders
Senior Editor Alexandra Andrzejewski
Art Director William Thomas
Senior Designer Jessica Lee
Decorative Illustrator Katsy Garcia
Portrait Illustrator Joel Kimmel
Proofreader Lisa Starnes
Indexer Celia McCoy

First American Edition, 2021
Published in the United States by DK Publishing
6081 E. 82nd Street, Indianapolis, IN 46250

Library of Congress Catalog Number: 2021930991
ISBN: 978-1-6156-4997-6

For the curious
www.dk.com

Contents

Boss, and Not Burnt Out

I've always had an entrepreneurial spirit. As a child, my sister and I typed up newspapers and sold subscriptions to our neighbors. In elementary school, a friend and I created a very thrifty business of selling acorns (complete with birth certificates) to classmates during recess. (This was banned by the teachers pretty quickly, but I swear we were onto something.) Both of my parents started their own businesses as well, and it was so helpful for me growing up to see adults create their own careers.

THE SEED OF A BUSINESS

Thinking maybe at some point I'd want to be an entrepreneur, I enrolled in Georgetown's undergraduate business school program. I wrote my entrance essay about starting my own stationery line which, come to think of it, is something I'd still love to do. But I always had the sense entrepreneurship wasn't something I'd do until I was well into adulthood, with college behind me and some work experience under my belt. I saw myself taking a more traditional path for a while and then, when I felt comfortable, I would maybe try to do my own thing.

However, there I was in 2008—my freshman year. At the end of the first semester, I was in my dorm room, overwhelmed with school, and, very frankly, wanting to drop out. The economy had crashed, and business school (with a huge emphasis on graduating and working in finance) didn't seem to make as much sense as it did when I applied. Somewhat randomly, a friend suggested that I start a blog, simply as a creative outlet...and the rest, as they say, is history.

For a couple of years, my blog was just that: a creative outlet. It was a bit of a lifeline, which also turned out to be a timely side project given the shifting economy. During the four years I was in college, the business program transitioned from a focus on finance to a focus on entrepreneurship. I happened to be studying the theories of business while running one from my own dorm room. I could take what I learned in the classroom and apply it to what I was doing with my blog. Oftentimes what was happening with social media was outpacing what my textbooks offered at an alarming rate.

Over time, though, what started as a creative outlet certainly became a job, both in the sense of the work I put in, as well as the income I received.

After graduation, I took a job with a startup in New York City. When I realized I was spending most of my waking hours building *someone else's* company, I wanted to give myself a shot and see what would happen if I devoted my time to my own business. I quit the startup—and haven't looked back!

BURNOUT

I have found a not insignificant level of success over the last decade, but it wasn't without some frustration and failure. What I consider my biggest failure may surprise you. It was *my mindset.*

When things switched from a creative outlet to a business, I went into overdrive. As a student, I barely slept. I was in classes all day, then in the library for studying and group projects, and then traveling to NYC nearly every weekend. I'd squeeze in my blog work whenever I could, which usually meant after midnight and before my alarm for the morning went off. It was even worse when I was living in the city and working at my first job. I was very much burning my candle from both ends—all in the name of the *hustle*. (This time was when "girl boss" and "#hustle" were all over Pinterest.) I felt like I was failing myself by not trying to do it all, all the time. I thought I was supposed to feel exhausted and burnt out. The less I slept, the more successful I thought I must be because it meant I was working all hours of the day. I fed off this energy and saw my exhaustion as a strength, not a weakness.

And then, when I was in my mid-20s, I quite literally hit my breaking point. All those years of #hustle caught up to me, and my body revolted. Only then did I realize how dangerous my mindset had been. I wasn't sleeping enough, I wasn't properly fueling my body, and my anxiety had never been worse. After spending a night in the emergency room, I vowed I would make the necessary changes to my lifestyle. I realized that I had to, or else I wouldn't survive.

BECOMING MINDED

Even still, I did this thinking I was trading success for a healthier lifestyle. I was, after all, still confident that it was the health sacrifices I made in the beginning that helped me achieve my level of success. It took a couple of years for me to shake that feeling, when I had a light bulb moment. I was healthy (and more importantly *happy*) *and* reaching more goals in a shorter time frame! I went from thinking, *I wouldn't have been as successful without giving up sleep and my overall health* to *How much more successful could I have been had I taken care of myself from the beginning?*

I had it wrong all along. There are countless things you need to know to create a healthy, profitable business, and it's just as important to make sure you—the entrepreneur—are a healthy and happy leader.

YOU COULD HAVE THE BEST IDEA IN THE WORLD, BUT IF YOU'RE NOT ABLE TO EFFECTIVELY RUN THE BUSINESS, IT CAN'T SUCCEED. YOU ARE YOUR BUSINESS'S GREATEST ASSET.

PASSING THE TORCH

I love helping people flesh out ideas for their businesses and work through problems, no matter where they are in their journey. My hope is that this book helps you hone your ideas and feel more confident making decisions, without forgetting to take care of yourself along the way.

Business Minded is divided into two parts. The first helps you set up your business for success, and the second helps you ensure that, as an entrepreneur, you're able to run your business in a healthy, mindful way.

As you work through the exercises in the book, I share helpful information to decode confusing terms and intimidating concepts, and also provide you space to map out your business. Best of all, there is a healthy dose of inspiration and insights from other entrepreneurs.

–CARLY A. RIORDAN

PART 1 Business

DREAM

FORMALIZE

STRATEGIZE

GROW

APPEAL

The Big Idea

Businesses come in all shapes and sizes. Everything we touch, use, need, and rely on is somehow rooted in a business. There's a huge spectrum. An idea for a business can be flashy and get the attention of investors who want to be involved in the next best thing. An idea can also be super simple, possibly even boring or mundane, but it solves a problem that excites you.

THE VISION

Because starting a business is not a one-size-fits-all situation, it can feel intimidating. There are endless businesses you can start, and endless ways you can pull off each one. There's no magic yellow brick road to follow that will guarantee an easy route—let alone success at the end. This is where that entrepreneurial spirit kicks in; part of the fun, even when it's not so fun, is figuring it out!

Usually a business starts with an idea. It can come to you in a dream. Maybe it's a product or service that solves some kind of problem. Maybe you already have a business that you want to take to the next level. You could have an inkling of an idea you want to explore to see if it's a viable business idea, or you could be starting from square one, knowing you want to start *some* kind of business but not knowing what that is. You may envision your company scaling and employing hundreds of people, or you may see yourself as the sole employee.

It's also totally possible that an idea for a business kind of fell into your lap. That's what happened to me when I started my website. I started it for fun, and over time, it became clear that I could actually turn it into a business based on what was happening in the industry around me— I stumbled into the idea.

IT DOESN'T HAVE TO BE PERFECT

No matter where you're starting off, there can be a lot of pressure around coming up with a great idea. If you struggle with perfectionism, you may think your idea needs to be completely fleshed out and perfect from day one. Try your best to relieve yourself of that pressure. Your idea doesn't have to—and probably won't—come to you overnight, and it certainly doesn't need to be perfect right away. *Relax.* You will not have to pitch your idea immediately to a team of investors. You're allowed to go in one direction and pivot down the road. You can change your mind completely. Once you start a business plan, you may realize that your idea, although great in theory, will be hard to pull off, and that's okay! Give yourself permission to give an idea a shot and see where it goes.

IDEATION TIPS:

- **Don't forget to keep track of your ideas.** This workbook is a great place to start, but you may not always have it on hand when an idea pops into your head. Writing down an idea helps commit it to memory. Keep a note on your phone, or send yourself an email as a reminder. Then you can add it to the workbook when you're back in front of it.

- **Keep your idea to yourself for a while.** If you're super excited about something, it can be hard to have your idea shot down by a friend or family member. (I have been there, and it can be incredibly deflating not to have support when an idea seems great to you, but others don't get the vision.)

- **Listen to your intuition.** Light bulb moments *can* happen, but don't be worried if one doesn't occur. It may be more of a lingering dull glow that you keep returning to in your mind. If you can't get it out of your head, explore that idea first!

A GOOD IDEA:

- **Excites you!** You can have a fantastic idea that you know will be a great business, but if it doesn't excite you, it's probably not worth exploring. Let someone else scoop it up. Creating and then running a business is hard enough when you love an idea—it'd be torture if you didn't.

- **Feels right.** This is a little more nuanced, but it's a bit like dating. Sometimes it just "feels" right. Don't worry if you can't quite put it into words just yet. The business plan you work on will help illuminate and define what makes the idea a winner.

- **Doesn't need to be fully fleshed out.** As you start working through your business plan (page 26), you'll have the chance to better hone in on your idea. You don't need to have everything mapped out from square one. Don't worry!

My Vision

USE THE JOURNAL LINES TO RECORD YOUR THOUGHTS TO THE FOLLOWING PROMPTS.

1. Take an inventory of things happening in your life. Is there a problem you think you could solve? A pain point you wish you could ease?

2. Have you and your friends been talking about something in particular that stands out as a potential business?

3. What skill do you have that could pivot into a business?

4. Is there something missing in your town or city that you would want to see brought to life?

5. Would you want to partner with a friend and combine both of your skills and passions into a business?

6. Consider previous jobs you've held. Were there aspects of those jobs you thoroughly enjoyed that could be a business?

7. Are there products or services in your life that could use a modern refresher?

8. Does something already exist that you think you could do better?

My Ideas

Possible Business Names

ENTREPRENEUR:

CARLY A. RIORDAN

Business name: TCP

Business description: I'm a full-time blogger, and I share a little bit of my life, a little bit of my style, and everything in between.

How long have you been in business?
I started my website in 2008 and turned it into a business, officially, in 2011.

Where are you headquartered?
Madison, NJ

How many employees do you have? 1 full-time (me!) plus a handful of contractors

How did you come up with the idea for your business?

My business idea was purely happenstance. Originally, I started my blog as a creative outlet while I was a freshman in college. It turned out to be the perfect time to start a blog because social media was rapidly developing into its own industry. I was lucky enough to be on the ground level of this and could ride the wave as it grew over time. I had no idea there would be a point in time when I could make money—let alone a full-time income—off of my website and various social media platforms. As I started to make money, I realized I needed to incorporate and legitimize my business so I could properly pay taxes on the income.

Have you had any additional business ideas over the years?

A ton! About once a year, I think I come up with a business idea that could potentially be worth pursuing. Sometimes I file it away for the future, and other times I tentatively see if it's worth my time and energy immediately. I have to admit that more often than not, my subsequent ideas have failed, or I have realized that I don't have the time to run my current business at the same time as another. However, I do feel like there's always a wheel turning in the back of my brain waiting for the next big idea to hit!

When do you know that you have a good idea or if one needs more work?

I definitely fall into the "fail quickly" camp. If I feel like a business idea might be worth something and it's something I don't want to wait on, I jump right in and try to figure out logistics. It's the best time to make hard decisions because there's less on the line when you're simply in a brainstorming phase. In the past, I have considered doing a line of stationery/paper goods, a clothing line, and a curated monthly gift-box subscription.... For different reasons, I realized each wasn't actually the right idea for me or the right idea for me at that time. They might be lack of resources (time, money, energy) or lack of passion (like when I realized I had no interest in managing anything with inventory).

What advice do you have for someone who desires to become an entrepreneur but doesn't have that "big idea" yet?

Keep your eyes and ears open!!! I highly recommend journaling— it could be a typical journal or a note you keep on your phone—and keeping track of any and all ideas. Look around your life and see what problems you, your friends, your family, and your neighbors face. Think about things you wish were done differently or products/ services you wish existed but don't. And don't forget to factor in your unique skill sets and interests. You might be able to offer something to the world that other people can't do themselves!

Hobby vs. Business

Once you have your big idea, it's worth spending the time now figuring out whether you want to pursue that idea as a business. I know, I know. You picked up this workbook because you *want* to create a business! Maybe you even picked up this book with the intention of figuring out how to turn your hobby into a business.

PERMISSION TO DO WHAT YOU WANT

It's incredibly important to know that when you create a business, it's not always rainbows and butterflies. It *will* be work. At some point, it *probably* will feel like the fun was sucked out of something you once loved. I'm not writing this to deter you from starting a business. Clearly this is something that can absolutely be worth your time, but it will benefit you to sit down before you start said business and come to terms with the fact that you're turning a hobby into work.

I want you to know, you have permission to keep your hobby *a hobby*. You do *not* have to listen to outside sources who tell you over and over again that you're so talented, you should sell your art! You don't have to take your passion for baking and start a food truck. You can love designing clothes for yourself without creating a clothing line.

There is joy in hobbies. You can find joy in making money from your hobby, or you may be content to keep doing it just for fun, but you can also strike a balance between the two. What you decide is up to you…there is no right or wrong way to do it.

You have permission to keep your hobby a hobby! It's okay if you don't want to turn it into a business.

A CASE STUDY IN CAKES

I'm biased, but my mom is one of the most amazing women I know. Truly, I don't think she's ever had a conversation with someone who didn't walk away in love with her and her personality. She was the dream mom to my sister and me; she was the self-appointed announcer for our softball games, showing up with a boombox and a playlist of songs to play in between innings. She volunteered at our schools and was PTA president more than once. She also baked. *A lot.* There was always some kind of baked good on our counter when we came home from school. When my sister and I went off to college, a family friend asked her to make cake pops for a graduation party. Those 200 cake pops ended up becoming 200 edible business cards. Soon my mom was being asked by other families to make cake pops for *their* parties.

Twelve years later, and my mom has a hybrid hobby/business making cake pops. She loves what she does, but she would be the first to admit that baking for strangers isn't exactly the same as baking for fun. It still brings her joy, but at the end of the day, she has to deal with all the headaches that come along with having a business. She has to worry about customer satisfaction, inventory control, pricing, bookkeeping, scale, etc.

I, along with countless friends and family members, have pressured her into growing her business even more over the years. My mom knows she *could* take it to new heights, but she's happy where she is, still maintaining a balance of work and fun. She consciously chooses *not* to advertise. (Remember, her cake pops have built-in advertising because people leave parties and want to know how they can get their own custom pops!) She turns down orders if they're outside of the scope of what she's comfortable doing. My mom made it a business on her own terms and still kept some of the joy of her hobby in the process. (Which is great for me because whenever I go home, my mom is never sick of baking and is totally happy to make whatever I'm in the mood for!)

Ask Yourself:

Are you okay turning a passion into work? For example, you may *love* to paint, but if the thought of having to paint commissioned works that aren't your style or having to paint a quantity that burns you out makes you resent the business, then a painting gig may not be the way to go.

To Hobby or Not?

Will I be okay taking on work from clients that I'm not super excited about?

- ☐ YES
- ☐ MAYBE
- ☐ NO

Am I open to receiving negative feedback regarding my work or ideas?

- ☐ YES
- ☐ MAYBE
- ☐ NO

Is it possible to make enough money doing my hobby to create a full-time income?

- ☐ YES
- ☐ MAYBE
- ☐ NO

Do I anticipate it feeling like work when I am no longer doing it just for fun?

- ☐ YES
- ☐ MAYBE
- ☐ NO

Have I experienced an instance where I couldn't do my hobby under pressure?

- ☐ YES
- ☐ MAYBE
- ☐ NO

Am I open to the risk of losing the joy of my hobby?

- ☐ YES
- ☐ MAYBE
- ☐ NO

Really Think About It!

What excites me about turning my hobby into a business?

What fears do I have about turning my hobby into a business?

Is doing a hybrid hobby/business possible with my current life, or would I have to go all in from the start?

What kind of additional emotional outlets will I have if I turn my hobby into a business?

Do I feel a "calling" to take my hobby to the next level?

How do I anticipate I will feel if it doesn't work out?

{definition}
A *niche* is where your product or service fits within the market space.

Finding Your Niche

Before you dig in to the rest of the book, I want to encourage you to examine your idea and make sure you have found the best niche for your business. A niche is the space in the market where your business fits. One of the best ways to visualize this is to pretend that a grocery store is "the market." Where your product would be placed within that grocery store is its niche. There are sections for produce, refrigerated goods, frozen goods, dry goods, and consumer goods, and each of those sections is divided even further. For example, the frozen section has frozen fruits/vegetables, packaged meals, desserts, etc. Ice cream's niche is within the frozen desserts then. It will compete against other ice cream brands and probably even options like frozen pies or popsicles.

YOUR SWEET SPOT

Remember from *The Big Idea* (page 10) that there are endless options for businesses—they come in all shapes, sizes, and colors. It can be overwhelming to think about how your business fits within the larger market, but when you break it down to find your niche, you'll have greater clarity on the space within which you'll play. Knowing your niche will help you make all kinds of decisions related to your business, like how to price things competitively based on other products/services in that space, how and where and to whom to market, what makes sense in terms of diversification of your offerings, and more.

If you're reading this chapter and don't feel super confident in your business idea (or maybe haven't landed on an idea at all yet!), you may feel better starting with what niche you want to occupy. Once you have the niche, you can reverse engineer to find an idea or tweak your existing idea. It could be that you've always dreamed of starting a clothing company, or you're a mom with small kids and feel like your town is missing something for families.

Finding your niche is crucial as you begin to map out the beginning stages of your business. There are risks with having a business that's *too* narrow, and there are risks if your business doesn't have a defined niche at all. You want to find a sweet spot where you can feel confident in creating a business. Not only will it help with your development of your company; more importantly, it will help your future customers figure out exactly who you are and what you do!

When you're super excited about your business idea, you may be inclined to jump right in to planning to get things off the ground as soon as possible. But, again, don't overlook the importance of honing in on your niche. In addition to being something that can help you build the best foundation for your business as you start out, this step can also help you as you grow and scale. Knowing your niche *now* can help you strategically plan for growth in the *future*, because you can plan ahead for all of the ways in which you can scale over time. There's a lot to keep in mind when defining your niche, from how to make sure you're able to build a core audience who immediately understands what it is you do to whether your niche is profitable as is.

Let's expand on the idea that you're dreaming of starting a clothing line and you're going to start with a line of dresses. Your niche from the outset would be women's apparel. It may potentially be too limiting, although not entirely impossible, to have *only* one type of women's fashion. And it might be too broad to have a clothing line that also specializes in something outside of that wheelhouse, such as candles. In the future, you may want to expand to include women's accessories like handbags and shoes, or add in a line of menswear. This would be a great way to expand your niche without confusing or alienating initial customers.

5 Keys to Keep in Mind

1
You don't want your business's focus to be too broad or too narrow; there's a sweet spot!

2
Make sure your business name isn't too limiting for your niche and potential future growth.

3
Profitability is vital for your business's financial future: your niche should be broad enough that you can generate revenue that is sustainable for the product or service you want to sell.

4
You can start with one niche and plan for possible expansion later—but expansion should make sense and be cohesive with your original idea.

5
Your core customer base will be built off of your initial niche, so it's important to start where you feel most confident in gaining a loyal following.

Honing In

What products or services do you wish to sell from day one?

_____

_____

What category or categories in the marketplace do these fall under?

_____

_____

Who do I want my initial core customer to be?

_____

_____

How could I potentially _narrow_ my business's niche?

_____

_____

How could I potentially _expand_ my business's niche?

_____

_____

What is my niche _not?_

_____

_____

Do I plan to expand my niche as my business naturally grows?

_____

_____

Would my core customer base change based on future expansion?

_____

_____

Is my business's name too limiting? How could I tweak it so I can expand my niche in the future?

_____

_____

ENTREPRENEURS:

CHRISTINA LIVADA & BETH LASALA

(daughter-mother duo!)

Business name: CHAPPYWRAP

Business description: We design and sell high-quality, cotton-blend blankets that are machine-washable, durable, super cozy, and made to last a lifetime. We say we're on a mission to spread comfort with the world's best blankets.

How long have you been in business? Beth founded the company in 2006. Christina joined full-time in 2018.

Where are you headquartered? Portland, ME

How many employees do you have? 4

What was the inspiration behind fleece blankets versus other materials or other home products?

Believe it or not, our blankets are not actually fleece! Fleece is a manufactured fiber—our blankets are made from a high-quality, natural cotton blend (58% cotton, 35% acrylic, 7% polyester), which is what sets them apart from a lot of other blankets on the market in the U.S. ChappyWrap was inspired by a family blanket my mom (Beth) grew up using and then passed down to my brother and me (Christina). It was so soft and durable and was clearly made to last. It was the blanket everyone always fought over, no matter how many other blankets were in the house. It was the first one we grabbed for when we were sick or sad or just needed that perfect couch nap. We all loved it so much, and when my mom went to try to find another one like it years later, she realized they are not available on the market in this country. The large majority of blankets here are made out of 100 percent manufactured fibers (100% polyester or polar fleece). This often means they don't wash well. They pill and fuzz and unfortunately don't last long. On the other end of the spectrum are super-high-end products made out of materials like cashmere, wool, or alpaca—blankets that are very expensive, dry-clean only, not super comfortable or warm, and not versatile for real-life use. One hundred percent cotton blankets are beautiful, but they lack the cozy factor because they don't provide a fluffy, soft feel and turn very flat after washing. When Beth realized this about the blanket market, she saw how ChappyWraps would fill a major void. They are comfortable, soft, warm, high-quality, machine-washable, and made to last. We loved the role the original blanket had played in our family; it held so many memories for all of us. We wanted to share that blanket experience with as many families as we could, and ChappyWrap was born!

Have there been specific challenges you faced for this particular niche?

It was initially challenging to find a manufacturer who could support this dream and who valued quality as much as we do. We have since found one and have a wonderful manufacturing relationship! Also, because it is such a tactile product you often need to experience to understand, it has been challenging to tell our story effectively and really communicate the magic of our product to people who have not felt it or used it before.

Do you have plans to expand into other items, or have you found this niche to be a good fit so far?

We do! We are launching our first nonblanket product soon and have more to come in the future.

What has been a key in ChappyWrap's ability to stand out among competitors?

I think the idea of family and home is what is truly unique about our product and our story. We are family run, and the idea was born because of something that was central to our home. We hear from so many customers who tell us that their ChappyWraps make them feel at home no matter where they are (traveling, in a dorm room, in the hospital, etc.), which is our company mission and makes us so happy! People begin to associate our blankets with home and comfort and security, and this is the exact experience we are trying to re-create and share with people. We also keep quality at the center of everything we do, which we think our customers recognize and appreciate.

What advice would you give to someone struggling to find the right niche for their business idea?

I think it really needs to be authentic and genuine. Is this a product that fills a void and solves a problem for you and other people in your life? Do you find yourself using it and needing it? How does it change your life? If you are passionate about it in this way, you will be able to tell that story and explain your emotional connection to the product, idea, and brand, and it will, in turn, feel and be authentic.

Creating a
Business Plan

I am sure you have heard about business plans. They are usually step one of starting a business. They are the thesis of what your company plans to do and are often used as a presentation for potential investors so they know who you are, what you plan on doing, and (most importantly) how you plan on making money. I can't recommend this exercise enough, even if you never intend on sharing your plan with anyone.

THE OUTLINE

Think of a business plan like the detailed outline of an essay. Yes, I know. I remember how annoying it was to preplan my essays for school. I always wanted to dive right in and start writing, kind of hoping (and praying) the paper would make complete sense by the time I got to the end. But I also remember how *crucial* it was to spend the time up front to come up with the best plan of action for the paper. Writing the outline would allow me to determine my thesis, ensure I had enough talking points to support my thesis, and find my initial research to make sure my talking points could be backed up with facts. Taking the time before I started gave me a leg up, and I always ended up with a stronger paper with less time wasted along the way. (I can't tell you how many times I thought I had a great idea until I got to the outline and realized it was going to be next to impossible to defend my thesis over 20 pages!)

{definition}

A *business plan* is a written document that outlines the who, what, where, when, why, and how of your business.

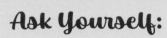

Ask Yourself:

When will you write your business plan? The answer to this question can help make sure your business is *truly* something you're passionate about. If you can't find the time, energy, or excitement to plan out your business, it's probably not the right one for you! A business plan seems difficult and confusing, but it's just the warm-up for running one!

The same is true for your business. By taking the time up front to plan out your business, you will be able to save yourself from huge potential headaches down the road. It will help you further flesh out everything we've already covered in this workbook and make sure you have a viable, profitable business on your hands.

WHAT TO INCLUDE

In your business plan, you will introduce who you are (if applicable), give a top-level brief on what your business will do, give a description of your company, provide a comprehensive market analysis, lay out how your company will be organized internally, describe what your company's product line or service will do, explain what your marketing and sales strategy will be, elaborate on how you will fund your company, and finally make financial projections.

There are some general rules of thumb to follow when you're creating your business plan, but how it looks at the very end can vary from business to business. You can get fancy and create a perfectly color-coordinated, flashy PDF that's pages and pages long that you'll bind and slide across a table for investors…but if it's for your eyes only, a handwritten plan in a journal can get the job done, too. Yes, if other people are going to see it, making a professional-looking document will help make a good first impression, but don't feel like you have to go crazy with it if you're only doing it as an exercise for yourself.

The Parts

1. PERSONAL INTRODUCTION (if applicable)

To begin your business plan, you want to open with who you are. This is where you "pitch" yourself to investors on why *you* are the best person to lead the charge on this business. Include relevant education, work experience, and personal passions.

2. EXECUTIVE SUMMARY

Give a top-level brief on what a reader will find in your business plan. Consider this the "thesis." State what your business objectives are, why you believe you will be successful, what the strategy is, and bottom-line financials. You want the reader to get excited about your company so they just *have* to know more.

3. COMPANY DESCRIPTION

Get a little nitty-gritty, sharing what kind of legal business you will set up (*Keeping It Legal, pages 32–35,* goes into this more) and why. Explain what exactly you will sell, to whom, and why.

4. COMPREHENSIVE MARKET ANALYSIS

Go into detail about what the market looks like. Find competitors, see what they're doing, and explain how you can improve on that and add differentiation.

5. COMPANY ORGANIZATION & MANAGEMENT

Explain what your company's organization will look like, and highlight key hires. State specific qualifications you and team members have to show why you're best for the job. Include all hires, including executive level, consultants, seasonal workers, freelancers, etc.

6. PRODUCT/SERVICE

Dig into exactly what it is you are going to sell, whether it's a product or a service. How will you create the product? What does research and development look like? Be as specific as you can in describing your product.

7. MARKETING STRATEGY

Map out your strategy for marketing the product. It will likely be a multitiered approach, so break it all down. Don't forget *who* you will target, *where* this will happen, and *how* you plan on doing it.

8. FUNDING

Walk through how you plan on funding your company from the beginning. (This is probably one of the most important sections.) It could be as simple as bootstrapping with savings to needing rounds of investors. Be specific with how you'll allocate initial funding.

9. FINANCIAL PROJECTIONS

Use this section to prove the viability of your business by demonstrating its profitability. Take into account expenses, and show revenue over time.

Business plan structure recommended by U.S. Small Business Administration.

The Mock Pitch

Even if you don't plan on sharing your business plan with outside investors, it's helpful to plan a mock pitch with a trusted friend or mentor. Walking through your plan, out loud, can help you get critical feedback from an outside perspective. Make sure you not only answer the questions your audience may have, but also ask *them* questions to ensure the plan is as clear as possible.

QUESTIONS TO ASK AFTER THE PITCH:

- Was there anything confusing in this pitch?
- Do you feel confident in what I pitched?
- If not, where could I provide more clarity?
- Is it clear what I'm trying to sell?
- Do you have a good understanding of how my company will stand out among competitors?
- Did my financial projections make sense?
- What section felt the strongest? The weakest?
- Should I add any information to make my pitch better?
- Was there anything in the pitch that didn't feel like it belonged?

QUESTIONS I RECEIVED & NOTES FOR RESPONSES

ENTREPRENEUR:

CHLOÉ WATTS

Business name: CHLOÉDIGITAL

Business description: chloédigital is the leading tech partner for influencers building content-based businesses globally. The community of influencers has access to strategic guidance, product development, and technical support to help them scale.

How long have you been in business? December 2014

Where are you headquartered? London

How many employees do you have? 15

You have created such a unique business in a new, growing industry. How did building a business plan help you get off the ground?

My business evolved organically in the blogging space, as the demand for technical knowledge was high. I had friends who had started blogging and needed support understanding the technical aspects of running and growing a blog. I am a developer, so I had the skill set to support them technically but also had the ability to translate technical jargon in a way they could understand, so they gravitated toward me. This soon evolved into chloédigital, a membership service that offers ongoing tech support and digital strategy for influencers. My business has adapted and reinvented over the years to the company it is today. I must confess, I didn't make a formal business plan at the start of this journey. However, as the business grew, I did then see the necessity to evolve and change when needed, and at these new turns, I created plans for each of them.

Have you had to go back and revise your business plan as your business grew and evolved over time?

I have constantly reinvented my business, and although the core values and my mission have remained unchanged, I have adapted my business to stay relevant and valuable in the market. At each point when I have added a new product, offer, or element to my business, I have taken the path of a business plan. This has given the wider team a clear goal for revenue, objectives, and deliverables while also allowing for flexibility and evolution.

If a new entrepreneur doesn't want to invest the time up front in creating a business plan, what would you tell her to encourage her that it's worth the time?

I didn't write a formal plan at the start of chloédigital, as we met demand and learned along the way, but looking back, I think a simple structure of what we wanted to achieve, the why, and revenue goals would have given me a clearer path in early entrepreneurship. It is also a great working guide to turn to when anyone, whether a partner, customer, or team member, requires more knowledge on what the business has set out to and can achieve. There are also other elements in play as to what the best approach is. If you are looking for early investment, then potential investors will want to see a pitch, which is essentially a business plan. If you are bootstrapping your business, like I did, you don't necessarily need to deliver a plan to anyone, but the benefits of investing the time to do this can be huge for maintaining focus and direction. Business plans have become hugely beneficial for me as I have evolved my business and given myself and my team a clearer path to success.

Keeping It Legal

One of the best things you can do for yourself *now* is to make sure everything is legally buttoned up with your business from the start. It is always easiest to do this from the very beginning, really before your business is off the ground and running.

COVERING YOUR BASES

Legally incorporating right from the get-go can ensure you don't have any headaches down the road. I know I'm guilty of saying I'll do XYZ later and then a year goes by and I still haven't dealt with it. Incorporating your business provides legal protection for your personal assets, as your business will be one entity that is separate from you personally. If you were ever to get sued, for example, it would be toward your business, and you and your personal assets (your bank accounts, your real estate, etc.) would not be liable for any damages. This protection is called limited liability (in contrast to unlimited liability, where your personal assets have no protection).

FINDING LEGAL HELP

This is where I personally felt the most stress when I was taking my blog (which was very much a hobby) and turning it into an incorporated business. Chances are, you've never done this before. It can sound like a foreign language, and you may not have a law degree to help you through the more minute details of setting up a legal business.

There are a couple of reasons why I recommend doing this early. The main one doesn't even really have anything to do with your actual business concerns at the moment. The exercise of getting your business incorporated requires that you start a relationship with a legal expert from the beginning. Even if you never have to rely on that person or team ever again, at the very least you have that relationship established. Unfortunately, a risk with owning a business is that you could run into legal problems. (I know, I know, this is not so fun!) Don't be scared by this, but do have it in the back of your mind as a possibility. You don't want to run into a problem and *then* have to go scrambling to find legal help. It doesn't have to be a formal relationship (you certainly don't need to put them on retainer), but having that contact can ease your mind. If a problem pops up, you have a place to start.

There's no one right way to go about finding legal services. While you can use a search engine and read reviews online before landing on one, I always suggest starting with recommendations from friends and family members in your area who have started businesses themselves. Why reinvent the wheel? (And don't forget to pay it forward when you're off and running and a new entrepreneur asks for advice!)

Depending on the size and type of business you plan on starting, it is worthwhile to find a lawyer who fits your specific needs. There are firms that specifically help small businesses and new entrepreneurs. If you're going to be starting a larger organization with more moving parts, it would make sense to find a firm that can handle your specific needs.

Choosing Your Business Structure

There are different implications for each type of business structure. This section helps you decide how to incorporate your business, but you will also want to seek additional advice from a legal expert to ensure you're making the best choice for your specific business needs.

SOLE PROPRIETORSHIP

If you do nothing, your business defaults to a sole proprietorship. If you don't want to spend any money and just want to start doing business right away and see how things go, this is your option. The most important thing to note, though, is that your business assets and your personal assets have no separation. So if you did get sued, for example, you'd be personally liable.

PARTNERSHIP

This is the most straightforward setup if you and another person (or group of people) are starting a business together. There are typically two kinds: limited partnerships and limited liability partnerships. In a limited partnership, only one partner has unlimited liability, and the others have limited liability (and usually less control of the company). In a limited liability partnership, each partner has limited liability.

LIMITED LIABILITY COMPANY (LLC)

If you register as an LLC, your business assets and personal assets are completely separate. With an LLC, you don't have to pay corporate taxes (your profit or loss can pass straight through to the individual level), but you are considered self-employed and subject to self-employment tax contributions.

C CORPORATION

A C corporation provides the most protection to owners, as it is a completely separate legal entity. There are more hoops to jump through (like more extensive record keeping and reporting). C corporations pay taxes on their profits, which can mean you get taxed twice because you pay the corporate taxes as well as individual taxes on dividends paid to shareholders. This is a good choice to make if you plan on eventually going public.

S CORPORATION

An S corporation is a unique form of corporation that allows profits and losses to be passed directly to shareholders, thereby avoiding the double taxation C corporations face. There are certain restrictions to who can form an S corporation, like having fewer than 100 shareholders and all shareholders must be U.S. citizens. You have to file specifically with the IRS to gain an S corp status.

B CORPORATION

A B corporation is similar to a C corporation in how it is taxed, but the corporation must have a commitment to some sort of public good in addition to financial gains.

NONPROFIT CORPORATION

A nonprofit is organized to do something to benefit the public, like charity, education, religious, literary, or scientific work. It follows similar rules to C corporation but receives tax-exempt status.

To-Do List

- [ ] Ask friends and family for recommendations for legal services.

- [ ] Set up meetings with a few legal teams to feel out needs.

- [ ] Make a decision on which team to go with.

- [ ] Set up a first meeting to get aligned.

- [ ] Determine how you want to incorporate your business.

- [ ] Choose and register your legal business name.

- [ ] Register with federal agencies (e.g., for your federal tax ID).

- [ ] Look into specific laws for running a business in your state.

Financing

Regardless of the size of your company, there will likely be *some* kind of expense, so you will need money up front. There are tons of different kinds of companies you can create, and that means there are tons of different ways and degrees in which companies can be funded.

INITIAL CAPITAL

Before you commit to one way of financing your business (see *Ways to Fund Your Business, page 39*), you should have a good understanding of what kind of capital you will need up front, what your financial projections will be over time, and what your immediate and future goals are. This is all information you likely have included in your business plan (page 26). If not, you can go back to your plan and add it.

It's my personal philosophy to try to avoid using other people's money, a.k.a. OPM. When you're using OPM, it's almost never a gift. At some point, they expect to be paid back with interest. They could be a bank or a group of investors, or even your family members. (Did your parents ever help you set up a lemonade stand when you were a kid, and the revenue from your first few sales went straight to them to pay them back for supplies they purchased for you at the grocery store? It's like that, but banks and investors will feel like a lot more pressure!)

BOOTSTRAPPING

I also like to recommend that people try to bootstrap their business because when it's your hard-earned dollars and when they're not as abundant as someone just cutting you a large check, you appreciate every dollar you spend a lot more. When you have a fresh box of tissues, for example, you don't think twice about grabbing two to blow your nose…when you're at the bottom of the box, you may go so far as to rip one in half to make the box last longer. When it's *your* money, you are more careful with how much you spend *and* how you spend it.

Another added benefit of bootstrapping is that it allows you to more easily pivot your business strategy. You won't need to run any changes by investors. You can make quick, necessary changes and decisions as they come because you're fully in control.

Of course, bootstrapping is not always an option, especially if you have big dreams and plans right from the get-go. Your company may require a big influx of cash from day one, and you may not always have that sitting in a savings account somewhere. You may need cash to invest in a brick-and-mortar lease for your restaurant. Or you may need cash to invest heavily in up-front costs to produce inventory for your clothing line. In these cases, you would have to seek capital from outside sources.

Again, there is no one right way to do this, and all entrepreneurs are going to be in their own unique financial situations, building their businesses with their own unique financial needs.

Understanding Your Financial Needs

Every business owner is going to have their own set of financial needs. You may need a big influx of cash initially, in which case going to an outside source for a loan may make the most sense. Or maybe you have a little nest egg that you've been saving just to get your dream business off the ground. Use this section to better understand what your financial needs will be to help decide which funding route to take.

What am I initially able to contribute financially?

_____
_____
_____
_____
_____

What level of risk am I willing to take: low or high?

_____
_____
_____
_____

What expenses am I responsible for before I am officially in business?

_____
_____
_____
_____

What expenses do I anticipate running into during the first year of business?

_____
_____
_____
_____

What are my financial projections? (Refer to your business plan.)
When will I start turning a profit?

_____
_____
_____
_____

Ways to Fund Your Business

SELF-FUND: If it's possible, the easiest and most straightforward way to fund a business is through self-funding, or bootstrapping. By bootstrapping your business, you retain complete control of the company.

SMALL BUSINESS LOAN: A lot of banks offer small business loans. There are different types of loans, and each has its own level of requirements and degree of lending available. When signing up for a small business loan, it's important to make sure you know exactly what the terms are.

REINVESTMENT: Reinvestment is a degree of self-funding but only applies if you already have some sort of business in operation. You might be branching out or expanding your current business, or this may be how you self-fund after you've already seen a degree of success.

CROWDFUNDING: This has grown in popularity in recent years and could be a fun and unique way to raise early capital for your business. It's pretty straightforward to crowdfund, and there are numerous websites that allow you to do so through social media. After setting a goal, you lay out your business (like a brief business plan) and explain what investors get in return for investing. One benefit of crowdfunding is that you can gauge interest in and excitement for your product or service (even getting crucial feedback in some cases). One drawback is that it requires some degree of an already built-in market or a way to tap into it.

GRANT: A grant is like a loan, but one you don't have to pay back. There are many kinds of grants, and it could be worth doing the research and seeing if you or your business qualify for any. There are grants given by the government (federal, state, and local levels) as well as by private institutions. For example, there are grants for nonprofits and businesses owned by certain demographics. While these are usually great opportunities, they can be time-consuming to apply for and quite competitive.

Bookkeeping

One of the most critical things you can do, starting day one of your business, is to keep good records of your financial situation. It is one of the least sexy parts about owning a business, but your future self will thank your current self for getting started now. Trust me on this. I think it's one of the biggest pain points for new businesses. There are so many things to think about when you're first getting your business off the ground, many of which are fun! And exciting! Especially if you're a creative person, you may be more inclined to focus your energy on perfecting your branding and making sure your product's packaging is "Instagrammable."

{definition}

Bookkeeping is the process of keeping track of all financial transactions for your business. Before computers, this was done by hand in physical books (hence the name). Now it's almost exclusively done digitally with computer software.

MAKE SMARTER BUSINESS DECISIONS

Being on top of your bookkeeping serves a few purposes. The first is that you'll use your books when you go to file your yearly taxes. You don't want to have to scramble at the end of the year to get everything in order. Every day that goes by, your business invariably has financial transactions occur—it's best to log these as they happen so you don't get behind. Additionally, when your books are up-to-date, you will be able to look at what's happening on any given day and know exactly where your company stands financially, which can help you make smarter and more informed decisions for your business.

Even if you are a creative person and not a numbers person, I encourage everyone who owns a business to be familiar with their books. Because it paints the financial picture of your business, it's vital that you know how to, at the very least, read your books so you can make informed decisions for your business's financial health. Even if it feels like a different language, keep with it. Your business will be better off for it! You can have the *best* product in the world, but if you're not able to make smart decisions, it could lead to poor long-term financial health.

HOW TO DO IT

If you've ever kept a personal budget, bookkeeping for your business is not so dissimilar. Bookkeeping keeps track of *every* financial transaction, including every expense you incur and every bit of revenue you take in. As you input the transactions into your books, you will categorize each one (e.g., advertising, insurance, sales, office maintenance, etc.). At the end of the year, you will know how much money you brought in, where you spent your money, and also what kinds of deductions you're able to take when you go to file your taxes.

Nowadays, there are many options you can use to keep track of your business's bookkeeping, from Excel spreadsheets (where you manually input) to computer software. There are free and paid options, and you should research your options to see what works best for your needs based on your confidence and the complexity of your business.

Terms

There are many terms used in bookkeeping. If you're not familiar with them, don't feel bad. It really can seem like a different language. When I was learning these in college, I felt so confused and in over my head. If you're reading this and feeling overwhelmed, too, rest easy. Once I started keeping track of my own bookkeeping for my business, it started to make a lot more sense. Here are some of the bookkeeping terms with which you should be familiar.

Account: All of your financial transactions are held in "accounts" within your general ledger. For example, you will have a Cash account where you track every transaction for which there is a change in your company's cash balance.

Accounts payable: Accounts payable are bills that you have been charged for but have not yet paid. These are what you owe vendors and suppliers. Accounts payable are recorded on your balance sheet and considered a liability because the transactions are debts owed.

Accounts receivable: Accounts receivable is money you have charged customers or clients for products and services that haven't been paid. Because the account is expected to be paid, this is considered an asset, or money earned.

Asset: Anything your company could convert into cash is considered an asset. This can be tangible items (like company vehicles) or intangible items (like a patent).

Cash flow: Cash flow is all of the money coming in and going out of your business—that is, the flow of your business's income and expenses.

Debit and credit: Put simply, when cash comes into an account, it is recorded as a debit, and when cash leaves an account, it is recorded as a credit.

Double-entry bookkeeping: With this method, each transaction is *always* recorded twice—once as a debit (cash coming into an account) and once as a credit (cash going out of an account).

Equity: Your company's equity is equal to your assets (that is, what you own) minus your liabilities (that is, what you owe).

Expense: Anything that you need to spend money on to keep your company running is considered an expense.

General ledger: This is where all of your company's accounts (also known as journals) are stored. Your general ledger is considered a complete record of your company's transactions.

Income: Income transactions are those that account for money earned by your company.

Journal entry: A journal entry is the chronological record of all transactions. A journal entry includes the date, the amount spent/earned, which

accounts are affected, and a description of the transaction.

Liability: A liability is what your company owes. This includes things such as unpaid bills, outstanding loans, and credit card balances.

Loss: A loss occurs when a company's expenses are greater than the income a company earns during a period of time.

Opening balance: This is the first transaction recorded in an account at the beginning of a new accounting period. The balance is carried over from the previous period.

Payroll: This is where you keep track of all of your employees and how much each is paid.

Profit: A profit occurs when a company's income is greater than the company's expenses.

Reconcile: In order to make sure your accounts are accurate, you must perform the accounting process of reconciliation. This ensures that the two sets of records are in agreement and equal.

Sale: Revenue your company earns through selling its products or services is recorded as a sale.

SAMPLE SETUP

With bookkeeping, it's important to choose a system that works for your particular business. Your books may not look exactly like another business's books, and that's totally fine. Here is one example of how a journal entry would look following double-entry bookkeeping.

Each entry includes the date, the amount spent/earned, which two accounts are affected, and a description of the transaction.

Date	Account	Description	Debit	Credit
1/21/2022	Office supplies	Pens and pencils	$24.30	
1/21/2022	Cash	Pens and pencils		$24.30

Here your entry shows that you purchased some office supplies with cash. The office supplies account gets debited $24.30 because it increases the value of the account, and your cash account gets credited $24.30 because it decreases the value of the account.

Accounting & Taxes

Similar to bookkeeping, accounting is one of the not-so-fun parts about running a business. Again, the language *can* seem foreign. (It absolutely was for me!) It can also be pretty daunting because the stakes are high. Accounting is what is going to make sure your business's finances are completely in order. This is helpful for running your business, making the necessary short- and long-term decisions, and filing your taxes properly.

DIY OR HIRE IT OUT?

This had always been my biggest point of stress because I feared messing up somehow and would have stress dreams the IRS was knocking on my door for an audit.

While admittedly not the most glamorous part of being an entrepreneur and potentially daunting if you're not familiar with accounting, it is absolutely doable. This is why staying on top of your bookkeeping from day one is so important—if you have your books in order, your accounting and your tax filing fall into place a little easier. Whereas bookkeeping is the day-to-day record-keeping of all transactions, accounting is the process of taking those transactions and turning them into readable reports. Those reports are then used to give an overview of how things are going financially across the entire organization. Business owners (and relevant stakeholders) can then use these insights to make various decisions. (These reports are also what you report to the government when it's time to pay taxes.)

Similar to my advice in *Keeping It Legal (page 32)* where I recommend finding a legal expert to help you, I would also recommend the same for your accounting and filing of taxes. I like to think that it takes all kinds of people to make the world go 'round, and there are people who eat, sleep, and breathe accounting. After attempting to file my own taxes the first year I was in business, I decided ultimately it was in my best interest to hire professionals. While this added an extra expense to my bottom line, I ended up saving money because they were able to look at my books and file my taxes in the most efficient way. They are also able to do much more than I can in way less time. Accounting and tax preparation are not my strengths, and outsourcing them allows me to spend my time where I work best.

BUT STAY ENGAGED

Now even if you *do* use a bookkeeper to manage your books and outsource your accounting, I still believe it's a good idea to know what's going on. The biggest reason for this? Understanding how to read accounting reports gives you a bird's-eye view of exactly how your business is doing at any given time. You may realize that while you're bringing in a ton of revenue, you're still not making a profit because your expenses are higher than what you're bringing in. Even if you're not the one running reports or filing the taxes specifically, you should be able to read the reports and understand what they mean and what they say about your business. In fact, I think it's so important, it could be worth taking a basic accounting course online just to feel a bit more familiar with everything.

Basic Accounting Formulas & Statements

Accounting equations and financial statements aggregate your business's financial transactions into usable information. These are the big-picture reports that can help you understand how your business is doing financially without having to weed through every little detail.

THE BASIC ACCOUNTING EQUATION

ASSETS	=	LIABILITIES	+	OWNER'S EQUITY				
ASSETS	=	LIABILITIES	+	CAPITAL	+	RETAINED EARNINGS		
ASSETS	=	LIABILITIES	+	CAPITAL	+	REVENUE − EXPENSES − DRAWINGS		

The basic accounting equation is the foundation of your business's accounting. It demonstrates the relationship among assets, liabilities, and owner's equity (all numbers you can find on your balance sheet). This helps ensure that your company's financial statements are, in fact, balanced.

BALANCE SHEET

This is one of the standard financial statements a business has. It can be run at any given time and shows what the business's liquidity is because it reports the overall assets (what the company is worth) at that specific moment.

ASSETS

Current Assets	Amount
Total Current Assets:	
Fixed Assets	
Total Fixed Assets:	
Inventory	
Total Inventory:	
TOTAL ASSETS:	

LIABILITIES

Current Liabilities	Amount
Total Current Liabilities:	
Long-Term Liabilities	
Total Long-Term Liabilities:	
TOTAL LIABILITIES:	
NET ASSETS:	

EQUITY

EQUITY:	
TOTAL EQUITY:	

PROFIT & LOSS (P&L)

The P&L, also referred to as the income statement, is one of the most important financial statements. It demonstrates, as the name suggests, the profits (or losses) a business is generating during a time frame. By looking at your P&L, you should be able to see what your revenue is and what your expenses are and look for ways to *increase* profit (i.e., increase revenue, decrease expenses).

COMPANY NAME
PROFIT & LOSS
1/1/2022–12/31/2022

INCOME	

E.g. Product sales
Service sales
Other income

TOTAL INCOME: _____

EXPENSES	

E.g. Wages
Advertising
Cost of goods sold
Rent
Insurance
Office supplies

TOTAL EXPENSES: _____

NET INCOME: _____

Pricing

No matter what your company is, by nature a business is in the business of selling *something*. It could be services, products, or a combination of the two. A crucial component of a solid business is having the right pricing for your products and services—you have to come up with some kind of price, or else you'd be in the gifting business, not the selling business.

Price your products and services too low, and you may not be able to make a profit (or worse, go into debt). Price your products and services too high, and you may not be able to get enough of an audience to buy into what you are selling.

Coming up with prices is both an art and a science. While at first glance it may seem that coming up with a price is simply a matter of math, human behavior interprets and perceives prices in unique ways.

THE SCIENCE

It's important to note that there are many different kinds of pricing strategies. I outline a few of those on page 51. Before you decide what kind of strategy you're going to implement, you should roll up your sleeves and dig into the numbers of your business. You need to know all the costs that go into making your product or running your service. In addition to calculating the cost of materials needed for each product or individual service, you should also take into account your business's overhead costs.

Let's say, as an example, that your business sells stickers of your own digital art. You need to gather the price of everything that goes into making each sheet of stickers. Figure out the price of ink used for each page and how much each individual sheet of sticker paper costs. You can't forget about how much it costs to ship and the price of the packaging (tissue paper, the plastic sleeve you mail it in, etc.). You should also have an understanding of what your rent, equipment, and labor costs are. If you know how much you expect to sell, you can divide those costs that go into making and shipping the product by the number of items sold.

From there, you need to consider what your markup will be. Because your costs only cover the expenses that go into your product, you need to increase the price so you actually generate a profit versus just breaking even. This is where those pricing strategies come in!

THE ART

Now, it seems like that would be a straightforward enough way of calculating the perfect price. Understand your costs, and then mark up the price enough to make a profit! If we lived in a vacuum, that would be enough. However, you can't discount human behavior and psychology when coming up with a pricing strategy. Enter: *the art!*

In the same vein as judging a book by its cover, consumers subconsciously judge products and services based on the pricing, which means you can influence how a consumer sees your product simply by playing with the price. You can price your product or service at a premium to demonstrate elite quality. You can entice consumers into thinking your product is a great deal by offering a discount (e.g., percentage off, buy one get one free, get 20% off your next order). You can even do something called *charm pricing* where you reduce the left digit by one. For example, charge $9.99 instead of $10 because the brain sees it as $9 not $10.

Cost Worksheet

Here's an example of how to calculate the various costs associated with your product or service. Of course, every product and service will differ slightly so you may have more, fewer, or different categories to consider.

CALCULATE THE COST OF THE PRODUCT OR SERVICE:

Price of raw materials or materials needed to perform your service:

$ _____

$ _____

$ _____

$ _____

$ _____

TOTAL: $ _____ ÷

number of units produced
or services provided

= $ _____   **cost per unit**

CALCULATE OVERHEAD COSTS:

Cost of labor associated with each product:

$ _____

$ _____

$ _____

TOTAL: $ _____

Cost of packaging and shipping expenses (if applicable to your product):

$ _____

$ _____

$ _____

TOTAL: $ _____

Cost of assets you will have to replace over time:

$ _____

$ _____

$ _____

TOTAL: $ _____

Common Pricing Strategies

There are many ways you can calculate pricing for products and services. It can be overwhelming, especially if this is the first time you're having to set a price. Again, there is an art and a science to this. It's worth looking into different models, playing around with the numbers internally, and conducting market research (like a focus group of your target audience) to see what price or price strategy makes the most sense for your product or service. Here are some common pricing strategies to get you started:

COST-ORIENTED PRICING:

This is the most straightforward pricing strategy and one that would be simplest to calculate (as we've discussed!). To calculate: COST + MARKUP = PRICE

MARKET-ORIENTED PRICING:

You may see this strategy called *competition-based pricing*. When choosing this strategy, you essentially look to see what competitors in your space are already doing. This could be a great place to start if your business is service based, where pricing is a little less cost driven. You have three options: price higher to signal to customers that you have a superior product, price lower to entice customers into believing in the better value of your product, or price the same to copy the market exactly.

DISCOUNT PRICING:

This is a common strategy you're probably very used to seeing on many websites. You artificially inflate prices and then offer a special discount, so it appears to be a great deal.

ENTREPRENEUR:

SARAH FLINT

Business name: SARAH FLINT

Business description: Founded in 2013, Sarah Flint is a luxury shoe brand based on the belief that women shouldn't have to choose between feeling good and looking great. Working closely with heritage Italian shoemakers, Sarah Flint combines traditional techniques with modern innovations to create footwear that's elegant on the outside and packed with comfort-driven design on the inside.

How long have you been in business? I founded Sarah Flint in 2013.

Where are you headquartered? New York City

How many employees do you have? 27

Coming up with a pricing strategy can be intimidating. Do you have a particular line of thought that you follow?

When I started my business, I looked at competitors and priced my line accordingly to make the margin I needed. Considering at this time I was selling through third-party retailers like Barneys and Bloomingdale's, I was required to price my shoes at an even greater markup. However, a challenge you have as a new brand is that you don't get the same volume discounts from your manufacturers because you are usually making your product in smaller quantities than the larger brands being sold alongside you. In essence, to compete, you have to price your products the same as your competitors, but your margins aren't as good because each of your items is more expensive to make. It's frustrating because not only are you less profitable, but because you're selling through third-party retailers, your product is also more expensive for your customer.

This realization—along with seeing consumer habits and spending shift increasingly to online—led us to rethink our business model and pricing. In 2017, we switched to a direct-to-consumer business, aiming for similar margins while occupying the white space in the market between contemporary and luxury-brand pricing.

What are some things you keep in mind as you set your prices?

I keep in mind what I think is missing in the market, which is a luxury good that sits in between contemporary and luxury-brand pricing. We want our prices to be more customer friendly, but still signal that our shoes are of the highest quality handcraftsmanship and thoughtful, original design.

Was there any point when you felt like you might have made a mistake while pricing items? Either too high or too low? How did you course correct?

It took us a little bit to get the right pricing balance between making our shoes more accessible than when they were sold through retailers, while still signaling all of the design and craft that is behind each style. At first, our pricing gave away too much margin, because without seeing our shoes in person or knowing our brand story, a customer wouldn't necessarily know the superior quality she was getting for that price point.

If someone is just starting a business today, what would you recommend as a first line of action for determining the best pricing strategy?

I think it's always important to look at the white space. Is there an area of the market that isn't being addressed? You always want to do what's best for your consumer and give them the best value you can.

Also, I think it's important to get an understanding, production-wise, of what your volume discounts will be down the road. If a certain price point is critical for your success, find out how you can get there with volume. An item will be less expensive to produce if you produce more of it, thus increasing your margins. Price for the long-term success of your business.

Inventory

Some businesses inherently are going to have to manage inventory. Your business may have a ton of inventory that you need to store in a warehouse where it will be distributed from, your business could have a small amount of inventory that is relatively easy to manage and keep track of, or you're somewhere in between. Understanding your inventory needs early helps you plan for financial success *and* can help alleviate headaches down the road. (It's important to note that if your company only provides intangible services or products, you likely will not have to worry about inventory or inventory management unless you offer physical products at some point.)

{definition}

Inventory is any physical product your company has on hand, including final goods ready for sale and any materials your business has that will be used for future production. Because inventory holds value, it is considered an asset of your business and is included on financial statements to reflect the value.

HOW MUCH TO KEEP ON HAND

Having a proper inventory strategy helps your business generate income efficiently, build customer satisfaction, and avoid unnecessary costs. Inventory holds a lot of weight and can be a risky portion of your business. Having too much inventory on hand can lead to unnecessary costs. Because inventory must be stored somewhere, you can accrue extraneous expenses associated with storage that could have been avoided. Inventory itself is expensive—remember, it's an asset—and by having too much, you may have allocated too much of your cash to inventory when it could have been used to cover other, more urgent expenses.

On the other hand, not having enough inventory to fulfill orders can lead to customer dissatisfaction. What happens if a customer comes to your store or website and the product they want is out of stock? They may turn to a competitor to get the item immediately instead of waiting for yours to come back in stock. Or, you may have too long of a lead time for delivery of the item, frustrating your customer while they wait.

The key is anticipating how much inventory you will need to have on hand at any given time and know when you will need to replenish inventory. With a proper inventory strategy in place, you will have better control over your cash flow (i.e., having money available so you can spend it when and where it needs to be spent); satisfied customers who can order your product when they want and have it delivered in a reasonable time; and an overall understanding of what product is available at any given moment, allowing you to make the best decisions for your company.

Inventory Terms

Here are some common terms and phrases you will come across while managing inventory. These may feel like foreign concepts if you're just getting started, but over time, you will become familiar with the terms as you roll up your sleeves and build out your inventory strategy.

Audit: An inventory audit is when a company compares financial records with actual inventory levels to ensure everything has been properly documented. Your financial records should always accurately represent the amount of inventory on hand.

Barcodes: This is a popular way of digitally keeping track of physical products. Each product has a barcode on it, and the barcodes are digitally synced with your inventory software. By scanning the barcodes, you can track and record inventory levels in real time.

Drop-shipping: This method of retail fulfillment is becoming increasingly popular. Instead of having to store and manage your own inventory, a third-party wholesaler or manufacturer handles the storing and shipping of inventory.

Finished good: A finished good is one that is completely made and ready to be shipped to customers.

First in, first out: As the name suggests, this is a method that ensures your oldest products are sold first. This is especially important if your inventory could expire or become obsolete over time.

Inventory turnover ratio: This ratio is how companies know how quickly they sell and replace inventory during a particular time frame. To calculate, divide the cost of goods sold within a period of time (on your P&L) by the average inventory during that time.

Point of sale: A point of sale (POS) is the transaction that occurs when your customer purchases something. (This could be in person, like at a checkout counter in a retail store or on an e-commerce website.) A POS system is the hardware/software system that tracks purchases and available inventory in real time across the board.

Quality control: This is the process by which a company ensures that all products on hand are up to acceptable standards. Quality-control procedures and testing likely occur at multiple points throughout the supply chain to ensure the final product meets predetermined product standards.

Raw materials: The raw materials are the individual components that go into making the final product.

Supply & demand: This is an economic principle of the relationship between the quantity of product a company has on hand and the quantity of the product consumers wish to buy.

Work in progress: A work in progress, or WIP, is a product that is in the middle of being produced.

Inventory Planning Checklist

Come up with an initial inventory strategy that makes sense for your business's needs and capabilities.

Determine where you will store inventory.

Perform an audit of the inventory you are starting with.

Identify your best (and worst) performing products.

Gather data on supply (what you are currently capable of producing) and customer demand.

Invest in and set up a POS system.

Prepare for a quality-control process.

ENTREPRENEUR:

SARAH ORTEGA

How did you come up with your current strategy for inventory?

I came up with our current inventory strategy based on years of testing, understanding market needs/trends, listening to customer feedback, and reviewing sales reporting to forecast our future needs! We have a few different categories that fall within our inventory strategy outlined below.

First, we have a focus on wedding and bridal jewelry, which includes engagement rings and wedding bands. From traditional to alternative styles, we design and offer a selection of rough- and fancy-cut diamonds alongside the more widely recognized white diamonds and sapphires.

We also offer other heirloom jewelry pieces made with semiprecious stones, which provide a more affordable option for customers and a great price point for gifting.

Lastly, we are known for our custom jewelry, which requires a slightly different strategy. We source stones specifically for these pieces from all over the globe, such as sapphires from Australia and lab-grown diamonds right here in the United States. I have built partnerships with various jewelers and suppliers over the last 14 years to ensure that all of the stones we use are carefully selected for their ethical and environmentally responsible origins.

What has been your biggest challenge (or lesson learned) regarding inventory management?

Navigating through 2020 definitely created some supply chain challenges and lessons learned along the way. We had store and jeweler shutdowns and canceled gemstone shows, which impacted our production timelines and inventory on hand. We also weren't sure if and how consumers would continue to spend on fine jewelry. All this

Business name: SARAH O. JEWELRY

Business description: Sarah O. is Denver's destination for unique fine jewelry and custom jewelry design. We offer ethically sourced diamonds, alternative gemstones, and locally designed pieces that fit a variety of styles, from traditional to alternative. We pride ourselves on providing a comfortable, inclusive environment for anyone who would like to browse our one-of-a-kind collections or set up a private custom-design consultation.

How long have you been in business? I started my first jewelry store called Ooh Aah Jewelry in November 2006 and opened Sarah O. Jewelry in April 2015.

Where are you headquartered? Denver, CO

How many employees do you have? 25

meant we had to really tune in to our audience and communicate clearly with them throughout the year. We were constantly pivoting based on the insights we were gleaning and managing expectations due to delays and/or changes in the process.

How have you managed the balance of having the right amount of inventory on hand?

To be honest, I am constantly learning the right balance of inventory, especially as a growing business! There are a lot of variables that go into inventory decisions. Sales reporting and production timelines play a big role, as well as customer trends (tracking of inquiries and what customers are asking for on social media). There are also outside factors like seasonality, holidays, and/or cultural events that we take into account.

What's interesting about our business is that similar to bridal gowns, a lot of our pieces are made to order, which can help with limiting the amount of inventory we need to have on hand. With that though, we are diligent when it comes to customer education and making sure people are aware of when they need to be placing orders so they get their engagement rings in time to pop the question!

If you could go back to the beginning of your entrepreneurial journey, is there anything you would do differently in regards to inventory?

At the beginning of my journey, I was buying based on my personal tastes and what I wanted, not what the customers wanted! Over time, I have learned the importance of customer feedback—whether it be about design, price point, etc.—and take this into consideration when coming up with new designs and our inventory mix.

Hiring

What happens when you can't do it all yourself? You may be faced with this problem before your business is even off the ground, or you may find yourself six months into your first year of business stretched so thin that you *have* to hire. There's also a good chance there are aspects of your business for which you're simply not the best person for the job—whether it's a specific skill set or you don't have enough hours in the day to do it all.

DELEGATE!

Every business is going to have unique hiring needs. One thing I see happen with small business owners is this need to try to do everything themselves. There's resistance to hiring because aren't we supposed to be able to do it all? I know that for years, I wore the fact that I did everything myself like a badge of honor. I wore every hat, even if the hats were too tight or too big. While I had a sense of pride from this, I shouldn't have. It led me to waste my time spinning my wheels on tasks that could have been done by someone else faster and more effectively.

I was also afraid of spending unnecessary money. Why should I pay someone to do a job that, technically, I could do myself? I slowly started to break down and realize how wrong I was. For example, it was taking me too long to file my taxes, and there was always the risk that I was going to mess it up somehow, as I was not and am not a tax expert. It was worth spending that money to free up my time, yes, but to also limit my risk of costly mistakes later.

Then I branched out and finally signed with an agency, where I had a manager to help

me with contracts and day-to-day communications with clients. This was what I was most resistant to because the agency would get a percentage of every contract I did. It felt like, although I would have less work to do as they took over all those communications, I would also make less money. However, once I had a team negotiating on my behalf who understood the market and knew what was fair and reasonable pay for these contracts, I was able to make more money on each deal. The difference more than covered the cost of having the manager helping *and* because my time was freed up, I was able to take on even *more* campaigns and make even *more* money.

It was such a mind-blowing concept to me at the time. Paying people to do what they're the best at helped my business's bottom line. Yes, I had greater expenses when paying a bigger team, but that bigger team allowed me to increase my revenue to a point that completely offset the expense— and then some.

And the best part? I could focus on the things about my business that I genuinely enjoyed doing!

Types of Hires

There are a number of types of employees you can hire. Each type has its own regulations and rules you have to follow (including "hiring" yourself!). It's important to know what rules you need to follow for each type of employee you hire depending on what state you live in, as it varies.

HERE ARE SOME COMMON TYPES OF EMPLOYEES:

SALARIED, FULL-TIME EMPLOYEES:

A full-time salaried employee works 40+ hours a week and is on payroll. Someone who receives a salary receives a fixed, regular income. For example, they are paid the same amount every two weeks. As a full-time employee, they are eligible for benefits such as health insurance, paid time off, etc. A full-time employee receives a W-2 form for taxes and is paid through your payroll, and the business must withhold and pay certain taxes.

PART-TIME EMPLOYEES:

A part-time employee works fewer than 40 hours a week. They are considered an employee of the company but are probably not eligible for benefits. A part-time employee is likely compensated an hourly rate (not salaried) through payroll and receives a W-2 form for taxes.

INDEPENDENT CONTRACTORS:

An independent contractor is someone who is self-employed but works on a contract basis for a company. Each contract has its own terms. The contractor may work for a specific period of time, or on a specific project, or be permanently contracted. Because they are self-employed, independent contractors are not eligible for benefits and are responsible for handling their taxes and managing expenses on their own. They receive a 1099 form for taxes.

INTERNS:

Offering internships has become incredibly popular in recent years. Interns may be paid, partially paid, or unpaid, mostly working in exchange for the experience while early in a career. (They're most common with high school students, college students, and people trying to break into an industry for a first job.) While unpaid internships are still happening, I recommend offering fair compensation for the work done, as accepting unpaid work is a privilege not every person is able to do.

Hiring Worksheet

Before you go on a hiring spree, there are some things to keep in mind when creating and filling roles within your company. Think about everything from immediate needs you have to how much additional revenue you expect from each hire.

What tasks do you enjoy doing yourself?

What tasks don't you feel qualified to do?

If you could take three responsibilities off your plate, what would they be?

Is there a branch of your business you want to focus on but don't have enough time?

Who is your "dream hire"? What qualities are essential to include in the job description?

Is there anything you would outsource immediately if you knew you could afford it?

ENTREPRENEUR:

JESSICA MEYERS

Business name: LYCETTE DESIGNS

Business description: Lycette is a family-owned needlepoint company dedicated to promoting the joy of needlepoint. We specialize in colorful, cheeky, and classic canvases that reflect our values of humor, beauty, community, and heritage.

How long have you been in business? 2016; first store in 2018

Where are you headquartered? Palm Beach, FL

How many employees do you have? 6

When did you decide it was the right time to hire employees?

I was frazzled, overwhelmed, and doing a lot of things rather poorly instead of doing a few things very well. A friend and fellow female entrepreneur stopped into the shop and recognized how exhausted I was. She told me that hiring turned her business around, that I needed to hire employees not only for my business but also for my mental health, and that I could call her with any questions. I knew it was time to hire once I realized how visible my exhaustion and frustration had become.

What were your biggest fears around hiring?

I was fearful of hiring employees who didn't align with Lycette's values or my work ethic (which happens). It is normal to initially hire people who either don't align with the company's values or are difficult to work alongside. Hiring is a skill set that is learned, usually after making a mistake or two. Instead of letting myself get to the point of exhaustion before searching for help, I wish I had initially invested time in writing down what my "ideal employee" looked like (values, communication style, etc.). Then, my preliminary hiring process would have been based around specific goals rather than a quick scramble to alleviate my workload.

As a small business owner, I was also worried about capital—how hiring would affect expenses. Obviously expenses increase when you invest in employees; however, hiring should be viewed as an investment. Employing competent and skillful workers allows a business owner to focus on areas of the business that they are passionate about, making hiring worth the cost of salary.

How has hiring/outsourcing/delegating helped your business?

It completely changed my business. When I hired employees, I was able to focus on the aspects of the business that I was good at and that invigorated me. Once I had the *aha* moment that I could, and should, employ people who specialized in tasks that I was *not* good at, such as organization and emails, it changed my business for the better. Yes, it is natural to have aspects of your job that are not invigorating; however, going to work shouldn't feel like pulling teeth. The more you can focus on projects that give you energy, the more you will give to the company, and the more people (including customers) will be drawn to your passion!

What was the biggest challenge around hiring employees, and what helped you overcome that?

Communicating expectations. Owning a small business continuously forces me to confront areas that I do not excel in, including straightforward communication. I have learned that unless you specifically ask an employee to do something or express how you would like a task completed, they will never meet your expectations. Employees aren't paid to read minds. Learning not only to identify what my needs and expectations are, but also to communicate those needs clearly and concisely to employees has been a challenge, and something that I work on daily.

What advice would you give someone running a business if they are scared to make the leap into hiring someone to help?

Take the time to sit down and identify what aspects of the business drain you and what aspects invigorate you. Hire someone for the tasks that drain you. Identify what your communication style is, and hire someone who works well with that. Imagine who your perfect employee would be, and put that in the job description. The more you identify what you are looking for and what you want done, the easier it will be to hire, and hire well!

Management & Leadership

It doesn't matter if you have one other employee or one hundred other employees, after you onboard the first hire besides yourself, you immediately have to start thinking about management! Even if you're not ready to do your first hires just yet, it makes sense to start thinking about and planning ahead for when or if you do.

TWO SIDES OF THE SAME COIN

Managing employees requires you to wear many hats. While it may seem like finding the right people to join your team is the hardest part, it's the first step of many! Successfully managing a team is no easy feat. I remember when I made my first hire, my first thought was, *Okay, now what?*

I would say managing employees is where I made the most mistakes when I first started hiring. I had managed a team before in a previous job, but at that time, I was also under another layer in the organization; so I felt like I had support to help me. Being a manager in my own business, I felt alone as I tried to balance being a good boss and managing the rest of the business. Setting the right tone of expectations was important from the beginning. I felt like I had to figure things out as I went, instead of taking the time up front to think things through.

A lot goes into properly managing a team of employees. Usually companies have specific departments that spearhead this (like human resources), so I think it's worth keeping that in mind if you feel overwhelmed. If you went into a bookstore, you would find an entire section dedicated to leadership within companies—countless books, theories, and courses!

Leadership and management, while intertwined, are also two separate issues. To have a successful and healthy team, you must be able to lead *and* manage. In your organization, you want to have everyone on the same page, working toward the same goal. Employees should feel both systemically supported within the company and inspired to perform well individually for the collective good.

Management is important for creating structure within your team and providing clear and concise guidelines. Leadership inspires employees to work together toward a common goal.

Management vs. Leadership

Think of management as the structure that employees need to feel supported within your company. A lot falls under this category, even though it's not as "sexy" as leadership.

- **Clearly communicate both expectations and responsibilities.** Your employees should know exactly what is expected of them and have a clear definition of their roles. This includes what they are responsible for and also what they are not. The clearer the better.

- **Properly train.** Even if it seems like a role is straightforward, there is almost always a need for some kind of training (or more complicated training if the role requires it). Your employees should be taught exactly how to do their jobs. It should never be assumed that they can do them the way you're expecting without guidance!

- **Set up support.** In a dream scenario, there would be no problems or hiccups. This is hardly ever the case. You should plan ahead for when issues arise. What should your employees do if they have an internal conflict? Who should they talk to if there is an issue that needs addressing? What will the protocol be for performance reviews?

- **Make an employee handbook.** Here, you can outline everything employees should know so there is never any confusion and they can reference it whenever they have a question.

Leadership is more of an art than a science. This is how you will inspire your employees to do and be their best. There are all kinds of leadership styles—it is worth taking into account your own personality and the vision you have for your company.

- **Lead by example.** Leading by example is probably the lowest-hanging-fruit style of leadership you can do. If you expect your employees to show up on time, you should show up on time. If you want your employees to have a healthy work/life balance, you shouldn't be at the office 24/7 and sending emails at 3 a.m. expecting immediate responses. Because your employees will look to you as the leader of an organization, you can set the tone simply by what you do and how you act.

- **Encourage ownership.** One of the best ways to inspire great performance and commitment is to ensure your team members feels like they have ownership in the company. While they don't have to have an actual financial stake in the business, they should feel like they are an important and vital part of the organization. Employees should be encouraged to share ideas and offer constructive criticism, all while feeling like their voices and opinions truly matter.

- **Be clear about goals.** Not only should your entire team be aware of company-wide goals, but everyone should know and feel like they are crucial in achieving them. Most organizations have different departments, but it's important that each department knows how it supports the others and vice versa. It takes a village!

- **Celebrate wins.** Don't just hit goals and then move on to the next. Make sure each "win" (big and small) is celebrated. It shows appreciation for the work that went in to get there and motivates employees for the next goal, knowing their achievements won't go unnoticed.

Creating a Company Culture

Company culture has certainly become a hot topic in recent years. Like leadership, there's a lot out there on what it takes to create a great company culture. I highly encourage everyone, regardless of company size, to think about what they want their company culture to be. Your organization will have a culture no matter what—it will naturally occur. If you are not consciously building and creating that culture though, you won't be in control of what it looks like in the end. (For example, without putting bumpers up to encourage healthy work/life balance, you may inadvertently create a culture where people feel pressured to respond to every 2 a.m. email within an hour... which can lead to overall employee dissatisfaction, high turnover, and burnout.) Get ahead of it by molding the culture you want from the start. Here are some questions to help you get there:

How do you want your employees to feel every day coming into work?

_____
_____
_____

Are there issues that you would like to avoid from previous experiences?

_____
_____
_____

What are some healthy boundaries you can encourage?

_____
_____
_____

What is an element of fun you can bring into the workplace?

_____
_____
_____

Are there practices you can bring into the daily schedule that inspire overall wellness?

_____
_____
_____

What is an element of health you can bring into the workplace?

_____
_____
_____

What have you liked about companies you worked for or ran before?

_____
_____
_____

What leadership traits and values do you wish to personally embody for your employees?

_____
_____
_____

ENTREPRENEURS:

SARAH PIERSON & ALEXA BUCKLEY

If managing a team doesn't come naturally, what tips would you give an entrepreneur to feel more comfortable in this role?

Clear communication and course setting are two key functions of leadership, no matter your management style. There is no one way to lead—both because each leader has different strengths and weaknesses and because each team member responds differently to management, motivation, and feedback. Understand your blind spots. Know your strengths. Know your team members' blind spots and strengths. Empower your team by giving them mastery and autonomy in pursuit of the goals that you set together.

How did you determine what kind of leadership style you wanted to implement?

We launched Margaux straight out of college at 22 years old, with so much to learn about business and life in general. Because we started the business when we were so young, we learned to lead by intuition—and by observing how others we admired led. At Margaux, leadership is about accountability, honesty, and most importantly, empathy. As a small, all-female team that has worked together for years, we are invested in each team member's personal and professional growth—and we believe it's so important to enjoy the journey, celebrating both wins and learning moments along the way.

Did you make a conscious effort to create a company culture? What values did you want to incorporate into the fabric of the culture?

We do make a conscious effort to create a company culture. We believe that it starts with a focus on the customer: who is she, where is she going, and what can we do to make her

Business name: MARGAUX

Business description: A modern woman's footwear business dedicated to making shoes as beautiful as they are comfortable.

How long have you been in business?
Launched May 2015

Where are you headquartered?
New York City

How many employees do you have?
6 employees, and additional employees in retail

life better? These values—and a commitment to doing best by our customers—permeates everything we do. Our customer-first culture is rooted in a commitment to quality, a focus on comfort, and a passion for telling the stories of the women who inspire us and our brand.

As your business grew, what challenges did you face in regards to management of employees?

As our business has grown, we've encountered two challenges: maintaining culture and aligning each member of the team on a singular set of goals. As we're still a small team, we've taken both as opportunities. Culture is ever evolving—especially in the present moment—but we also believe it starts with our customer. By keeping our customer at the forefront of everything we do, prioritize,

and consider, we unify the team around a singular focus and mission. And if we're unified on this mission, then it is much easier to align goals. We set quarterly and annual goals as a team and review our progress on a monthly basis. We also share our individual priorities for the week with the team every Monday and report on the progress of each on Fridays. We've learned that alignment comes from strong communication, so creating regular space for this communication in our team calendars has been an enormous unlock.

{definition}

Branding is a broad term indicating how you represent to the outside world what the core of your company is all about through design, logos, and messaging.

Branding

Branding is a critical element of your business. Often it's the first thing potential customers judge you on. They can't get a peek into your financial statements. They don't know how you've structured your business or how you file your taxes. They don't know how many employees you have, or what your distribution center looks like. But when they come to your website, or view your newsletters, or walk into your store, or scroll through your social media accounts, they can get a sense of who you are.

WHY IT MATTERS

When you have a powerful brand strategy, potential customers get a sense of what makes your business great, what core values you stand for, and the personality of your company. Branding helps you differentiate yourself from competitors and leaves a lasting impression on your customers.

There are new businesses popping up every day, and with that comes an increased level of competition and a lot of "noise" as every company tries to get the biggest share of the market as they can. You might have the best product or service in your industry, but if you can't get the right attention from the right customer, it doesn't matter. When done well, your branding can help you stand out among the crowd. I'm sure you can think right now of a few products that you've picked up or tried solely from the branding. Have you ever walked through a store and found yourself reaching for a bottle of shampoo just because the label had a sleek design? Without knowing anything else about that shampoo, the branding alone compelled you to give it a try!

HOW TO DO IT RIGHT

Coming up with a brand identity can be an expensive endeavor. Branding has blossomed into its own industry, and firms can charge high rates to help you hone in on your company's identity. If you have the cash, it may be worth working with professionals to establish a brand from the very start. Because branding is such a valuable element of your business, if you can, it's worth doing it right and immediately starting to build brand awareness and brand loyalty from customers. Especially because there is increased competition with a booming e-commerce industry and the rise of social media, having a killer brand can be incredibly powerful in helping to get your foot in the door, and (importantly) converting sales.

With that said, if you are just getting started and don't have that kind of liquid cash ready to go, you can absolutely do it yourself by brainstorming and following some simple rules of thumb.

Whether you're using a firm to help you build out your brand identity or you're doing it yourself, don't rush the process. It's crucial that you get your branding right from the start. The adage *measure twice, cut once* comes to mind. A rebrand (that is, changing your already established brand) can be costly and requires significant resources. You will have to invest your time and money, not only in the creation of the new branding, but also in remarketing and rebuilding awareness of the new brand so you don't lose customers in the process.

Understanding Your Brand Identity

Here are some prompts to help you sharpen your company's identity.

What is your company's mission statement?

_____
_____
_____
_____
_____

Describe three or four of your ideal customers.

_____
_____
_____
_____
_____

Name your company's core values.

_____
_____
_____
_____
_____

How do you want customers to feel when interacting with your brand?

_____
_____
_____
_____
_____

List a few adjectives to describe your company's personality.

_____
_____
_____
_____
_____

Who are three of your main competitors?

_____
_____
_____
_____
_____

Who is your target demographic?

_____
_____
_____
_____
_____

What differentiates your company from competition?

_____
_____
_____
_____
_____

Visual Branding

Once you have an understanding of your brand identity, you can start to transform that into a visual representation that will become your branding. Reference what you have established as your brand identity when making your choices for visual branding. For example, if you see your brand as fun and youthful, your selections should also feel fun and youthful, and if you see your brand as elevated and classic, your selections should also feel elevated and classic. The goal is to create the visual representation of your core brand identity. Use these elements as a template to get you started.

Consistency is key. You want to use the *same* branding elements across the board.

MAIN LOGO

PHOTO INSPIRATION

SECONDARY LOGO/ICONS

MAIN & SECONDARY COLORS

PRIMARY & SECONDARY FONTS

ENTREPRENEUR:

CLAIRE ORING

Business name: OUI CREATE

Business description: We're a creative studio that produces commercial content for clients around the world. We specialize in short-form creative assets like stop-motion animation. We love creating studio and lifestyle content for the "finer things in life," from fancy champagne to delicate perfumes to luxe home goods. We try to infuse a bit of magic into each project!

How long have you been in business?
Since 2019

Where are you headquartered? Los Angeles

How many employees do you have?
3 day-to-day, but we pull in up to 7 contractors monthly for various projects. Usually working with about 10 on our team monthly.

You have such a distinct branding style for your own business. How do you think this helps you stand out among competitors offering similar services?

When running a creative agency, I think it's so important to have a strong point of view in your marketing. It proves to your clients you can do the same for them in their own style. I find lots of junior designers share any work that comes through their pipeline, and they get stuck in a cycle of never leveling up because they attract the same level clients from the work they are sharing.

We are very specific about the portfolio content we share because we are always trying to level up and attract our true dream clients. We only post content in line with our goals, which means holding some of the content we work on monthly. To attract the high-end clients we want, we only share our best work in line with our goals and really focus on speaking directly to them so we continue to pull in more clients and brands that are in the exact verticals we want to work in. So far a couple years into business, this has helped us pull in some legit luxury brands like Absolut Vodka, Sofia Rose, Tocca Perfume, Almay, etc.

Why do you think having a strong and unique visual identity is so important in today's market?

Branding is not just a logo slapped together with Canva. It should be an experience for your audience. Every touch point should be curated to express your unique point of view and attract your ideal client. Having a unique point of view is vital. As a designer, if you are truly unique and have your own aesthetic, no one can do what you do—and you can charge whatever you want. YOU are the magic sprinkled all over your work, and clients will want it for their own.

What branding mistakes do you see companies frequently make, and how should entrepreneurs avoid those pitfalls?

In today's digital market, everyone is pulling inspiration off Pinterest and Instagram, and so many aesthetics are blending together. Not to say everyone is copying each other, but many businesses' branding tend to fall into a few basic buckets that everyone pulls from. I would challenge business owners to look for inspiration off social media to avoid blending in.

Here are a few ideas:
- Art history and architecture.
- Vintage magazines (I buy them at flea markets or on Etsy) and books.
- Music! If you could turn your favorite song into something visual, what would it look like? I bet a Mozart symphony would look pretty different from the latest K-pop hit.
- Travel—how can you not be inspired by a new culture or city?
- Playing with time—pulling from the past or imagining a new future.

Do you have a tip or two for helping entrepreneurs hone in on their own branding styles for their businesses?

When a client or customer looks at your work, how do you want them to feel? That's probably the most important question to keep asking yourself during a branding project. You have the ability to curate their experience and warm up their imagination over the course of their time with you. Attention spans are so short; make your visuals captivating so they stick around longer.

And a final tip: fake it 'til you make it! If you are a brand-new company or even a side hustle, having legitimate, professional branding establishes you so much faster. Clients who land on your page will take you seriously regardless of your stage of business because it's kind of hard to tell from the outside how long someone has been in business. So buttoned-up, thoughtful branding will really help you excel at a faster pace.

Marketing

Simply put, marketing is how a business promotes itself to appeal to new customers and retain existing ones. Marketing has come a long way in the digital age, and it's easy to think that social media is the only marketing tool worthwhile, but that's not quite the case. Marketing is a pretty big umbrella, and there's no one "right" way to go about it. Everything from commercials on radio and television, to postcards in the mail, to a guy in a hot dog suit outside your store all fall under the umbrella of marketing. It can be overwhelming knowing just how many options there are, but look at them as opportunities. There should be no pressure to try to do it all. With some strategic planning, you can narrow down who it is you are trying to reach and how you can best reach them.

Ask Yourself:

When coming up with your marketing strategy, ask yourself: *what* are you trying to sell, *who* are you trying to sell that to, *where* is that audience, and *how* do they consume information? Knowing all of this will guide your strategy so you can effectively persuade them on why they want/need your product/service.

WHAT, WHO, WHERE, & HOW

Your business may have a mix of products or services available, and you can—and probably should—have a marketing strategy for each, especially if the audience or use for each product/service is slightly different. When thinking of the *what*, break down your business's product and service offerings into individual or group segments, depending on what makes the most sense.

The *who* would be your target audience. Remember back to when you were first starting your company; you probably had an idea of exactly who you created the product or service for. It may have been new moms, busy young professionals, retired people with disposable income, people who work in a specific area, etc. Knowing and understanding your core customers helps you hone in on where they are, how they consume information, and what practice will help convince them that they need to try your product or service.

After you know the segment of people you're trying to reach, then you can research *where* and *how* these people consume information. This is crucial! When you know exactly where that audience is spending their time (whether this is a physical location or a digital space), you can make sure your marketing efforts happen in the right space.

Once you have the setup, then it's a matter of taking the highlights of your products and services, mixed with your already established branding identity, to sell that audience on your business. You'll want to present a compelling case through your marketing and branding that your products or services are the right fit for them. The ultimate goal is converting a sale!

Defining Your Audience

When determining your target audience, a helpful exercise is to come up with a *persona*. It's a fun way to conceptualize who it is you are trying to market to by building a made-up character who epitomizes that target audience. You are also not limited by just one persona. Remember that your products and services could target multiple audience segments. Because you want to market to those groups in unique ways that speak to them, it's worth building out personas for each segment. Use the questions below to get started building out your consumer profiles.

PERSONA

Name: _____

Age: _____

Sex: _____

Where do they live? _____

What is their job description? _____

What is their income level? _____

Are they married? _____

Do they have children? _____

What is their education level? _____

GOALS: What personal goals do they have? What professional goals do they have? What are they working toward right now and in the next five years? How would your product or service help them reach their goals?

VALUES: What values do they hold true? What is important to them? How do their values drive their decisions?

CHALLENGES: What challenges do they currently face in their personal or professional lives? Will they have new challenges pop up in the next five years? How do they address and handle their challenges?

LIFE: What activities do they participate in? Where do they go? How do they prefer shopping? Do they have hobbies?

Mapping Out Your Marketing Strategy

When mapping out your marketing strategy, you want to return
to the what, who, where, and how.

WHAT
You likely won't have a one-size-fits-all approach for each of the products or services you wish to market. When coming up with your marketing strategy, dive deep into what makes that product or service unique.

- What makes this product or service stand out among the crowd?
- What are competitors doing for the same type of product or service?
- What are some shortcomings of the product or service that may cause hiccups with marketing?

WHO
By now you should have a good understanding of the core customer or customers you are trying to market to.

- Use the personas you created to drive strategy.
- Consider setting up a focus group to better understand your audience. Make sure you have a full understanding and catch any potential holes.

WHERE
A key to marketing is to make sure that your marketing materials get in front of the right eyes! To accomplish this, you have to know *where* your audience is. This is a twofold question.

- Geographically, where are they, and how will that location factor into your marketing strategy?
- Digitally, where do they spend their time online? Think about social media platforms they belong to, websites they might visit, and e-commerce sites where they shop.

HOW
Once you know who your customers are and where they are, you have to understand and take into account how they consume information. Use this when creating marketing content and materials.

- Do they prefer traditional outlets like television, radio, or newspapers?
- Do they like modern outlets like social media, podcasts, and influencers?

Business name: GRACE ROSE FARM

Business description: The most beautiful roses in the world: fragrant, heirloom California-grown garden roses shipped nationally. As the preeminent supplier of cut garden roses in the United States, Grace Rose Farm is committed to ethically growing and harvesting over 60 varieties of heirloom garden roses. Gracie and Ryan Poulson, as owners and current stewards of the land, have spent years nurturing their soil and rose plants with organic and sustainable methods. The resulting blooms are revolutionizing the expectations for domestic cut roses. With innovative shipping materials and a commitment to customer service, roses are delivered to satisfied customers throughout the country. Gracie and Ryan, along with their team, deeply believe in the power of flowers to spread joy and bring people together.

How long have you been in business? When we purchased our first home in 2016, I had the idea to grow a rose garden in honor of my grandma. As a couple, we planted over 500 rose bushes. As they began blooming, I shared images of the unique varieties and colors on Instagram. Requests started pouring in from floral designers, and as we began shipping their roses locally and around the country, Grace Rose Farm was born. We've been in business since 2016!

Where are you headquartered? Our forever farm in Somis, CA, in Ventura County.

How many employees do you have? In all 31 people. We have 20 full-time employees on-site. Our IT, marketing, and PR teams (6 people) are offsite. Our 24/7 customer service is also offsite (5 people).

ENTREPRENEURS:

GRACIE & RYAN POULSON

What marketing strategies have you found to be most beneficial to your business? Gracie comes from a digital design/creative background, so she created our original collateral such as logo, website, and brand imagery. For us, branding and packaging are everything, and the unboxings people share on social media have been a huge part of our success. We are known for packing our roses so the experience of opening them is like Christmas morning. All the little details in the presentation matter so much. We also handwrite notes for each order—over 200 per day! Word travels fast when you employ old-fashioned touches like handwritten notes.

Social media has been an amazing avenue for us to connect with our customers. It is a little less formal, which we love! It also allows us to work with other small businesses. Collaborating with small businesses and influencers has been amazing for our business because our flowers are so easy to capture beautifully on Instagram for so many different uses. Social media has always allowed us to share more of the day-to-day farm life with our customers, and they absolutely love it. From rose-field tours, to the coolers packed with roses, to how we prune during winter— our customers enjoy being taken along for the journey! We've also connected with people by sharing our infertility and adoption story and personal life events on our blog.

Have you made any mistakes in investing in marketing that didn't work out? What did you learn from that?

We are pretty quick to steer the ship in a different direction when something isn't working for our business. Any marketing "mistakes" we have made in the past have ultimately led us to where we are now, and I am so grateful for that. Being able to pivot when things aren't going as planned is key to successful entrepreneurship.

Are there any tips you have for standing out among competitors when it comes to marketing?

Our owner/founder story is so unique, and there is no one in the United States growing and shipping heirloom garden roses like Grace Rose Farm. People want to know the story behind the business, so I definitely think sharing from a place of authenticity is the best way to truly stand out. Be unique, strive for transparency, use social media to connect (not just sell), and tell your story. A lot of companies

ship flowers, but no one else has our farm story and can show the abundance of blooms coming out of the fields. We strive to capture "farm to vase" in our messaging.

How did you define who your audience is, and how did you know how to effectively reach them through marketing?

We were originally selling to mainly event florists. Leading up to 2020, we coincidentally had begun setting up our direct-to-consumer capacity. That year, when everything changed, we were able to pivot immediately to retail, thankfully, because all events were canceled. Now, our main audience is retail customers, and reaching them with a product as visually stunning as our own has been a rewarding challenge. We have grown organically on social media as well as through a wonderful influencer program, and we spend quite a bit on Facebook and Instagram advertising that shows the farm and beauty we create. We also show our farm workers quite often, and people really love that. They love knowing who grew and packaged their flowers.

What advice would you give to an entrepreneur who doesn't know where to start with a marketing strategy for their business?

Invite your customers along on your journey, and show them the heart of your business so they truly know who they are supporting when they buy from you. Share your team and family with them, your goals and desires, glimpses of your life, and keep it as relatable as possible while also being aspirational and authentic.

Social Media

Social media has become one of the most important marketing tools at your disposal. Every single business, especially new ones, should be investing in social media marketing. It doesn't matter what industry you're in, how many people you employ, or what you sell, social media of some kind will be incredibly beneficial.

WHY INVEST IN SOCIAL MEDIA

For your business, social media is beyond just sharing pictures of avocado toast or throwbacks from your last vacation or silly dances with your friends. You can use it to establish brand awareness, showcasing to potential customers exactly who you are with branded imagery and messaging. You can use it to get feedback from customers and build a more personal relationship with top customers, making them feel valued and appreciated. With social media, you can drum up interest for upcoming products and services and even convert sales right through many of the apps. It's an accessible tool for marketing (of course), but also customer service, branding, sales, and more.

If you're starting a business now, be sure to put "social media strategy" at the top of your to-do list. It can feel overwhelming to dive into platforms, starting from scratch. One thing I hear from business owners is that cracking the code for building an audience from scratch nowadays is impossible. I'm here to tell you—it is not impossible!

START BUILDING & BE CONSISTENT

Should you expect your first video to go viral overnight or get 100,000 new followers in the first month? Probably not. Reframing your goals for social media can help you maintain realistic expectations and find success from day one.

Here are some ideas for *realistic goals* for your social media marketing strategy:
- Increase brand awareness
- Provide customer service opportunities
- Convert sales
- Get feedback directly from customers to improve product/service
- Reach new audiences
- Drive traffic to your website

The industry of social media itself is ever evolving, so it is important that you constantly revisit your strategy to keep it fresh and relevant. Every few months, it seems like a new platform pops up, and I know firsthand just how overwhelming that can feel. While I do think you should have a robust strategy, you may have to strike a balance if you have limited resources (time, employees, money). My rule of thumb here is to do as much as you can without losing out on consistency.

Instead of feeling like you have to do it all and be on every single platform, make an effort to be on as many platforms and post as frequently as you can *without* losing out on consistency. That could mean six platforms or two platforms, or simply one if that is what your resources allow.

Posting consistently on social media means a few things. First, this is where your brand identity comes into play. You should have consistent imagery, fonts, language, and messaging—all of this going back to what you already established as your brand. You should also post at a consistent frequency. If you can't post every single day because you don't have a dedicated team ready to handle the content creation, sit down to figure out how frequently you can post at regular intervals.

Creating Your Strategy & Goals

Sitting down and coming up with your strategy for social media and the goals you wish to meet helps ensure you're spending your time and money in the right ways! There are many directions in which a company can go, but streamlining the process keeps everyone on track.

Who will be running your social media accounts? What resources (financial, time, equipment) will that person or team have available to them? What will their responsibilities be (content creation, management, customer service, etc.)?

_____

_____

_____

_____

_____

What type of content or content mix do you feel best matches your brand identity (long-form videos, short videos, professional photography, quick snapshots, customer-created/submitted content, illustrations, graphics with text, etc.)?

_____

_____

_____

_____

_____

What are your main objectives for social media (create brand awareness, build customer loyalty, convert on sales, etc.)?

_____

_____

_____

_____

_____

When will you revisit objectives, goals, and strategy?

_____

_____

_____

_____

What platform(s) do you want to prioritize, and how do you plan on using those to meet your main objectives?

_____

_____

_____

_____

_____

Content Calendar

A content calendar helps you or your dedicated social media team plan ahead for what to post, when to post, and where to post it. Depending on your company's specific needs, the calendar could be simple and straightforward or incredibly robust. Not only is this a great way to keep track of what you have already planned, but it can help you find holes in your strategy. For example, you may determine you need to increase the number of photo shoots so you have more photographs to work with. Or you may realize you need to have a better line of communication with your sales team to know when big launches are happening to line up your content calendar.

MONTH

SUNDAY	MONDAY	TUESDAY	WEDNESDAY	THURSDAY	FRIDAY	SATURDAY
			1 10 a.m.: New launch 10 a.m.: New launch 10 a.m.: New launch	2	3 10 a.m.: Video 2 p.m.: New arrival link 6 p.m.: Reshare of launch	4
5	6 10 a.m.: Photo 2 p.m.: RT community 6 p.m.: Photo	7	8 10 a.m.: Sneak peek 10 a.m.: Sneak peek 10 a.m.: Sneak peek	9	10 10 a.m.: Photo 2 p.m.: RT community 6 p.m.: Photo	11
12	13 10 a.m.: Photo 2 p.m.: RT community 6 p.m.: Photo	14	15 10 a.m.: Sneak peek 10 a.m.: Sneak peek 10 a.m.: Sneak peek	16	17 10 a.m.: New launch 10 a.m.: New launch 10 a.m.: New launch	18
19	20 10 a.m.: Photo 2 p.m.: RT community 6 p.m.: Photo	21	22 10 a.m.: Video 2 p.m.: RT community 6 p.m.: Throwback	23	24 10 a.m.: Photo 2 p.m.: RT community 6 p.m.: Photo	25
26	27 10 a.m.: Photo 2 p.m.: RT community 6 p.m.: Photo	28	29 10 a.m.: Video 2 p.m.: RT community 6 p.m.: Coming soon	30		

PLATFORM ONE · PLATFORM TWO · PLATFORM THREE

Use your content calendar to keep track of important dates for your company (like product launches and special anniversaries) and national holidays (both nationally recognized and fun). Include specifics of what will be published, where it will be published, and when it will be published.

Social Good

While businesses are generally known for generating profit and creating jobs, they also have the ability to give back to communities either locally or around the world. Benjamin Franklin is often attributed with saying, "Do well by doing good." The idea for social good within business, also known as social enterprise, is very much in line with this.

A company that participates in social good is one that seeks to make a positive social or environmental impact in the world.

CONSUMERS CARE

The social good can be the entire basis of the company, like a nonprofit. Traditional for-profit businesses can incorporate social good and social responsibility into its overall mission, too. Social enterprise has become a more popular business model to adopt in recent years as consumers have become much more conscientious with their purchases. Young people in particular are thinking more about the businesses they support and the impact their dollar makes within a bigger picture.

This presents a great opportunity for your business and should be seriously considered. Even if your company is not a nonprofit fully dedicated to solving an environmental or social issue, incorporating some kind of social good into your business model can be incredibly beneficial for both your bottom line and your brand awareness.

Not only is it great to be able to contribute to a cause that aligns with your overall business, it can be a valuable tool for marketing as well. Having an element of social good attracts conscientious consumers (and conscientious employees).

POSITIVE BRAND AWARENESS

Especially as barriers to entry are lowered, making it easier for more and more people to start businesses, it can be difficult for new (and frankly existing) companies to stand out among competitors. Because more consumers are actively researching companies and paying attention to where they spend their dollars, creating a business plan that actively supports a social good can be that final hook that draws a potential customer away from a competitor and toward your product or service.

Because social-good models attract more customers, you can convert more sales, which in turn leads to a bigger impact for the social good. This is a win-win that should be celebrated! The better your business performs, the better your financial bottom line *and* the bigger the impact, environmentally or socially, you are able to make. If you're donating a backpack to a kid in need for every backpack that your company sells, the more backpacks you are able to sell, the more backpacks you are able to donate, which means a larger profit for your business, yes, but also more kids in need receiving backpacks for school!

Strategies for Good

There are a few different strategies for social good. If it's something you're interested in incorporating within your company, you can determine what's the best fit for how your company operates and what your main objectives are.

OPPORTUNITY EMPLOYMENT:

This is a multifaceted approach. A company engaging in opportunity employment may have a specific mission or take a broader approach. Some examples include actively recruiting from typically untapped employment pools, such as people seeking reemployment after incarceration or people with intellectual and developmental disabilities; providing wages that allow a person to support a family (also known as a "family wage") and benefits for all employees; or providing training that goes beyond the fundamentals to ensure equitable professional success for all employees.

DONATION BASED:

You are probably familiar with donation-based social-good initiatives. A company may decide that for every product sold, it will donate one product to an organization that aligns with its mission, or that a percentage of all sales goes toward some kind of environmental or social organization that, again, aligns with the overall mission of the company.

INNOVATIVE PRODUCT OR SERVICE:

Maybe the product itself is one that helps fight an environmental or social issue. Maybe you've found a way to reuse plastic to create a new innovative product, or you have a service that raises money to benefit a cause.

Brainstorming Causes

If pursuing a social good business model or incorporating some element of social good into your business strategy, it's important to choose the *right* cause with which to align. It should make sense to a consumer why you have chosen this particular cause. If you are creating a beauty product line for millennial women, donating shoes to children, while admirable, doesn't make a ton of sense on paper. Instead, maybe for every beauty product your company sells, you donate a personal hygiene product to an organization that benefits homeless women.

Who is your core customer buying
your product?

_____

_____

_____

_____

_____

What causes or organizations are important to
your core customers?

_____

_____

_____

_____

_____

What category does your product or service
fall under?

_____

_____

_____

_____

_____

Is there a cause or organization that directly
relates to the history or mission of your
company?

_____

_____

_____

_____

What kinds of environmental or social
categories make sense for your product
or service?

_____

_____

_____

_____

_____

What model makes the most sense for your
company (employment opportunity, donation
based, innovative product or service)?

_____

_____

_____

_____

_____

ENTREPRENEURS:

LAUREN STEPHENS & KAKI MCGRATH

Business name: DUDLEY STEPHENS

Business description: We make clothing from innovative recycled fabrics, thoughtfully designed by and for modern women, in addition to men and children. We are best known for creating a niche by connecting the warm and soft fleece fabric everyone knows and loves with the stylish, outfit-making silhouettes everyone wants. In addition to our fleece collection, we launched DS Beyond in 2021—our first expansion into recycled jersey fabrics.

How long have you been in business? We launched in 2015.

Where are you headquartered? Greenwich, CT

How many employees do you have? 12

In what way is your company committed to social good practices?

From the beginning, we knew that if there was a way to design, manufacture, and sell our clothing that would also make a positive impact, we would choose that path. To us, good social practices take several forms. First, Dudley Stephens sources only fabrics that are made using recycled materials: all of our fabrics were made using yarn spun from plastic bottles that would otherwise find their way to landfills and oceans. We also calibrate production to reduce waste and strive to design pieces that last season after season. We're selective when it comes to our fabric manufacturers—we like to work with like-minded suppliers—and support and collaborate with female-founded companies like ours whenever possible. We intentionally strive toward a diverse community of customers and partners, prioritizing diversity in advertising and marketing. We give back through brand philanthropy under our #dsgives initiative, providing financial and in-kind support via partnerships with St. Jude Children's Research Hospital and local organizations like Bundles of Joy.

Was this always part of your business strategy or something you added after getting started?

Yes, this was our mission from the beginning; the concept of stylish fleece clothing and the sourcing of recycled materials were always hand-in-hand ideals. We also believed that as women launching a company, we could be in a position to inspire, promote, and empower other women to pursue their own entrepreneurial ideas.

Is this a cause that was always important to you?

[Lauren] After working in the fashion industry for over 10 years and seeing firsthand how it was becoming possible to source responsibly without compromise, I knew that it was essential to join and lead a growing movement that could have a meaningful impact. We also wanted to design clothes for busy women who need their wardrobes to adapt to their multitasking lives—pieces that are durable, yet stylish, and that can be worn over the course of many years, well beyond just one season.

How have you found the social good element beneficial to your company over time?

It's been incredibly beneficial and well timed, as our community of customers has become far more aware of their shopping habits. They are much more conscious and inquisitive when it comes to where their clothing comes from, who made it, how long will it last, and what was used to make it—all questions we can answer with transparency and pride. Since 2015, we've grown a very loyal following and customer base that appreciate the brand's story and what we stand for; they are an integral part of our messaging and will continue to be for the future.

For entrepreneurs who wish to incorporate a social good component into their business strategy, what advice would you recommend they consider?

Be genuine in your messaging. Keep things simple and true to your core idea and values. Always start small—with one idea—and run with it. It's tempting to try to take on the world, but don't try to do it all at once!

Also, be open to constant learning. We are always developing knowledge about manufacturing, our supply chain, and the future of the fashion industry and how we can do better. The more we know, the more we realize how much is left to do. Recycled fabrics are just one step in the right direction toward creating a more circular economy. As we've learned, we've pivoted and no longer use the word *sustainable* in any of our messaging. We call our fabrics recycled because that is what they are. Claiming that you are sustainable as a company means so much more, and not many companies can truly make that claim. There is a lot of research and development being done right now in supply chains, manufacturing practices, and the circular economy. It is an exciting time to be involved and witness all of the new developments on the horizon and to play a role in some of them through Dudley Stephens.

PART 2 Minded

Working Smarter, Not Harder

This is one of my favorite personal mottoes. I use it as a mantra that I repeat to myself throughout the day, and I highly recommend adopting it yourself. After spending so many of the first years of my career burning the candle at both ends, it's sometimes hard to remember that it's not necessarily about the *hours* you put in. If I'm efficient and happy, I actually work a lot less in terms of number of hours, yet my output is both greater quality and less time-consuming.

IT'S NOT ABOUT WORKING HARD

To work smarter, we first have to dismantle the notion that you must work harder.

My father-in-law once told me a story that really resonated with me. We were on a family vacation, and I was struggling with a little guilt at having taken a full week off. I had brought my laptop with me, but had, so far, successfully resisted the urge to open it and respond to emails. While I expressed the guilt I was feeling, he told me about a famous American jurist who used to take an entire month off of work every summer to spend time with his family. He assured everyone in the office that he "could get done in 11 months what [he] could not do in 12." The idea here is that by taking off an entire month, he was actually able to be a better employee and deliver better work. If he didn't take that time off, he would have worked more hours and days, yes, but he wouldn't have had the same output without taking that break to rest and recharge.

I think about this often. The work culture in recent years has put a premium on "hustle."

But at what cost? It's as if there's an invisible trophy waiting for people to see who works the longest hours, responds to emails in the quickest amount of time (bonus points after midnight!), and takes the shortest lunch breaks. Spoiler alert: there is no invisible trophy waiting for you—just a high risk of burnout.

As an entrepreneur, you will always have something to do. There will always be decisions to be made, projects to oversee, fires to put out, growth to map out, et cetera, et cetera, et cetera. It is a trap to think you must be spinning your wheels all the time or trying to show off to your employees just how much heart you have in the game by working nonstop. (In fact, a good leader leads by example, and that means exhibiting a healthy work-life balance! You don't want to lose yourself *or* your employees to burnout!)

Working smarter means you're getting as much done, and probably even more, without drowning and losing yourself in your work.

Common Traps of Working Harder

A lot of what we believe to be the guidebook for excelling in the workplace can actually be a trap of working harder instead of smarter. We have been trained and groomed to feel the need to work *harder* and *longer* than everyone else. It might have been coached into you on a high school sports team where the kid who did extra weightlifting sessions was seen as a star player and praised for their dedication. (Never mind the fact that they injured themselves from overworking their muscles a week before the big playoff.) Or you may have been celebrated by your first boss early in your career for answering emails at 3 a.m. (Never mind that you quit the job after only one year because you couldn't handle the stress of the work environment anymore.) In a sense, it will require a bit of deprogramming to retrain your brain.

• • •

HERE ARE SOME OF THE COMMON TRAPS OF WORKING HARDER:

- **Not knowing what each day will bring.**
  >> Set a daily or weekly routine that you grow accustomed to.

- **Not having a proper end to the workday.**
  >> Find a time every day that makes sense to end working, no matter what.

- **Having three or four tasks occurring at once.**
  >> Just say "no" to multitasking. Give each task your undivided attention.

- **Doing all the work yourself.**
  >> Don't be afraid to delegate tasks that aren't your specialty to other employees.

- **Completing tasks as they come, in any order.**
  >> Prioritizing is key. Focus on the most important tasks first.

Opportunities for Working Smarter

Take some time to think about the instances in your workday when you could be more strategic about working smarter, not harder. I do not recommend trying to fill this out in one sitting, but instead take notes over a period of time. Look for moments in the day that fit into the *working harder* column that you would like to transfer into a *working smarter* moment. Whenever you feel like you're just spinning your wheels and not actually moving forward with a task, jot it down. Whenever you feel a moment of stress that disrupts your flow, take note of what happened, and so on. After the column fills up, set aside a chunk of time one afternoon (make it a meeting on your calendar so you stick to it) to sit down and brainstorm how those moments could be better.

WORKING **HARDER**	WORKING **SMARTER**
EXAMPLE: 3 p.m.: I found myself frustrated over a series of small events. I was angry and lost my cool with my assistant—only to realize I had skipped lunch due to back-to-back client meetings.	It's worth taking the time for lunch every day. I get to disconnect from work and come back focused and fueled. I am going to put a standing meeting on my calendar for 30 minutes every day to ensure I have time to eat.

ENTREPRENEUR:

DIANE HILL

Business name: DIANE HILL

Business description:
I make bright, bold, and uplifting art that aspires to bring style and sophistication to modern lives with pieces that make every day beautiful.

How long have you been in business? 2016

Where are you headquartered? United Kingdom

How many employees do you have? Just me and a brand-new part-time employee

You have described yourself as a "chillpreneur." What does that mean to you?

Being a chillpreneur to me is the sweet spot of building the best business possible, in the most economical and efficient way, and using the least energy. It's about delegating, automating, or eliminating. I learned this concept from Denise Duffield-Thomas, who has great advice for any woman looking to grow a profitable business, as well as enjoy life to the fullest and without neglecting their family. Twenty to thirty years ago, it used to be all about who worked the most insane hours, woke the earliest, and sacrificed the most. The internet has opened up new doors, especially for women. We now have the opportunity to bring our passions to life, share them with others, and work our own hours. We also have access to the best apps and software to make every aspect of our businesses easier. Then on top of that, we have been given so many free platforms to market ourselves without much professional marketing knowledge—although doing as much research as possible helps immensely!

What are a few examples of how you work smarter, not harder, in your business?

First thing for me, before I considered hiring anyone to help with my business, I looked at my home life to see how I could make that easier. I was finding that the biggest things getting in the way of me focusing on my work were looking after the children and taking care of the house. So the first tasks I outsourced were childcare and a weekly cleaner. That freed up so much mental capacity that even five years down the line, I have only just felt the need to employ someone to work with me inside the business.

Probably the smartest thing I have ever done for my business is having all of my orders drop-shipped automatically. This is a system where, when an order goes in through my website, the order automatically goes through to my art printer who also ships it straight to my customer. It means I do not have to think about anything. When I get an order I say, "Yay!" and then get back to painting more beautiful things. Prior to that, I had been packaging and shipping orders myself, and I can't tell you how labor-intensive that can be! This amazing system also saved me big time when I once got an unexpected 1,000 orders in a week when a charity art print of mine went viral. I probably would have had a breakdown if I had to fulfill them all myself. Instead, it was expertly handled for me.

I also take a couple of hours out of my working day to go to the gym, which may seem counterproductive, but it actually has the opposite effect: I can work harder for the remainder of the day because my energy comes from movement. I sleep in relatively late (until about 8 a.m.), take the kids to school, make breakfast, then go to the gym. Most days I don't start work until lunchtime (unless I have a tight deadline). It's great because I feel super relaxed and stress free, which makes for a much happier work life. I pinch myself some days at how lucky I am to live this way!

Have you had periods of time where you felt outside pressure to work "harder"?

I have been in business for five years, and four of those years were solely dedicated to solid mural and wallpaper jobs, all hand-painted bespoke work. These were the years when I felt constant outside pressure to work hard. Although I felt so lucky to be working for myself and growing my own business, I was also the most stressed I'd ever been in my life. I have only very recently pulled away from all

bespoke work. The pressure was too much to bear. I decided my life and my sanity were worth more. When working for high-end interior design projects, there are almost always tight deadlines, and I am the kind of person who would never dream of missing deadlines. So instead I would work myself silly to deliver on time; this was not sustainable and not the kind of life I wanted to live. It affected my family, too, which made everything worse. I am so pleased to say that I am moving forward on my own terms, running an e-commerce business from my home, in my own time.

What would you tell a new entrepreneur struggling to fight against societal pressure to hustle harder at the expense of their own well-being?

I could sit and talk to anyone for hours on end about this, as I am so passionate about it! Gone are the days when you have to pull all-nighters and sacrifice your personal life. We have been blessed with the facilities at the touch of a button to make following our dreams that much easier. It is never worth sacrificing your sanity for anything because you have one short life on this earth. I feel we are in quite an exciting time, particularly for women—we can work from home and on our own schedule. I know of successful businesses now that don't even have an office or retail location, and all staff work remotely. It's all about direct to consumer now, cutting out the stockists that reduce profit margins, and using social media to skyrocket your online presence without the need for the bigger players.

Planning Your Day

One of the best things you can do for yourself as an entrepreneur and a leader within your company is to plan your day as best as you can. You may be thinking, *But isn't one of the perks of working for yourself and running your own company that you can set your own schedule?* One hundred percent. But part of the perk of setting your own schedule is that you have to actually go through the process of setting the schedule.

YOUR *WHOLE* DAY

As an entrepreneur, it's a given that you will always feel like there is more work to be done. It can be an incredibly easy trap to fall into (i.e., working all the time because there is always work to be done) and an incredibly difficult trap to get out of (i.e., you will still always feel like there is work to be done, even if you worked every hour of every day). By setting a schedule and coming up with a daily routine that works for you—and eventually works for your team if you end up hiring employees—you can establish a healthy balance between work hours and nonwork hours.

There is a critical mindset shift you should adopt here. While it seems on paper that your nonwork hours are spent doing things, well, unrelated to your work, those hours *are* still important to your working hours. The time you spend with your family around the dinner table every night, the time you spend walking your dogs through your neighborhood, and even the time you spend watching television is important.

That's when you give yourself needed space away from your work. In that space, you have the potential to find clarity on problems you face at work, new ideas to take your business to the next level, and the overall happiness and well-being you need as the entrepreneur to lead business development.

Now, here is where the perk of building your own schedule returns. You do have a good bit of control over what that schedule looks like. If you're a mom, you may want to schedule your day to have a break between 3 p.m. and 7 p.m. so you can do school pickup and have dinner together as a family. Or maybe you are building this company while you also work another job, so your new business work schedule occurs between 6 p.m. and 10 p.m. during the week and Saturdays during the day. It will take some planning and prioritizing to make sure you're setting up an ideal workflow, both from a daily and then weekly (and potentially long-term) basis.

What Needs to Get Done

Every entrepreneur is going to have a different schedule. In a way, that can be challenging as you plan out how to spend your day. It took me years to fine-tune how I plan out my day, and I still have to go in and tweak it depending on my stage of life, my priorities at the time, and the scope of work that needs to get done over time. Don't feel like what you decide has to be set in stone. It should be a work in progress: set a schedule to create a routine, but don't be so rigid that there is no room for flexibility as you need to evolve.

The first step is understanding what you need—and want—to get done throughout any given day. Use this page to map out those priorities.

- I am a morning bird, night owl, or a mix: _____
- The time of day I feel most productive: _____
- The time of day when I find myself hitting a wall: _____
- The time of day when I have the least number of interruptions: _____

What do you want to accomplish every day outside of work (e.g., exercise, dinner with partner/family, an hour to read, etc.)?

_____

_____

What do you *need* to accomplish every day for work? (Make note of different needs throughout the week/month if applicable.)

_____

_____

What hours do you need to be available for work (e.g., time that you must work to overlap with employees, communicate with suppliers, be available for store hours, etc.)?

_____

_____

What hours do you want to block off for personal priorities (e.g., school drop-off/pickup, a standing weekly therapy session, etc.)?

_____

_____

Sample Schedule

There are myriad ways you can plan out your day, from apps on your phone that sync to your laptop to old-fashioned paper planners. Here is a sample way to set up your daily schedule. I recommend including absolutely everything you need and want to do throughout the day in one spot. If you want to accomplish it, schedule it.

DAILY SCHEDULE

S M T W T F S   DATE:

6 a.m.	
7 a.m.	
8 a.m.	
9 a.m.	
10 a.m.	
11 a.m.	
Noon	
1 p.m.	
2 p.m.	
3 p.m.	
4 p.m.	
5 p.m.	
6 p.m.	
7 p.m.	
8 p.m.	
9 p.m.	
10 p.m.	

TODAY I MUST:

-
-
-
-
-
-
-

TODAY I WANT TO:

NOTES:

ENTREPRENEUR:

SARA O'BRIEN

What do you take into account when planning out your day?

I have a structured plan (as much as can be) that highlights the priorities (phone calls, meetings, and deadlines, as well as family commitments like school events or kiddo appointments) and allows flexible time in between to tackle the day-to-day happenings that can flow more easily from one to the next.

Do you have any secret tips or hacks for planning an effective workday?

I must have a to-do list. I use a basic lined notebook...and a massive wall calendar! I write through my tasks by hand so they sink in!

Do you ever feel pressured that you need to work all the time? How do you incorporate values outside of work (family, working out, relaxing, etc.) into your daily schedule?

At times, 1,000 percent! As I grow older, though, I'm learning to find balance wherever I can between work and family life. I think the truth is, you're always leaning in one direction or the other...and maybe that's the key to it all: the back and forth, the overall balance. After days that feel full to the brim with work commitments, we'll take a family beach walk or watch a fun movie together. We also try to involve our children in Sara Fitz projects whenever we can, sharing

Business name: SARA FITZ

Business description: We're a New England–inspired design brand offering multiple lines of delightfully illustrated goods.

How long have you been in business? July 2016

Where are you headquartered? York Harbor, ME

How many employees do you have? Currently in flux! We've worked hard to curate a small but mighty team of vendors and manufacturers who share our brand's vision. Miles O'Brien oversees general business operations, including all aspects of our wholesale and trade divisions. I [Sara] focus on the creative—illustration and design, brand collaborations, marketing, styling, and so forth.

ideas for new products or artwork. They enjoy being part of it all, and we love to watch them take pride in that!

What benefits have you found for your business and personal life from scheduling your days the way that you do?

I find myself truly savoring both my business and personal life as we grow our brand. For me, there has been something freeing about letting myself rise and fall like the tide. Some days, weeks, and months are literally nonstop—and instead of fighting to control them, I embrace the chaos and I count my blessings. And then, of course, when I have quality time with my boys (which luckily is still often as they're both fairly young), I soak it in, knowing it's fleeting and life is much too fast!

What advice would you give to an entrepreneur struggling to effectively plan out her day?

FOCUS. It can be too easy to get sidetracked by time-consuming tasks that don't make much difference to your bigger picture! You've got to trim it down! Figure out where your priorities are, and always head toward them. If you feel overwhelmed, break your picture down a bit, unfold the layers, and tackle one thing at a time. There's no shortcut, but you'll be moving in the right direction!

Setting Goals

As an entrepreneur, setting goals can help you make sure you're staying on track for the big picture. When you're starting a business or running an already successful one, it can be so easy to get caught up in the mundane, everyday elements. By setting both short- and long-term goals, you will be able to have a bird's-eye view of your personal and professional lives and make sure you're heading in the direction you wish to go.

THE BEST MOTIVATOR

As an entrepreneur, your brain may want to jump immediately to setting goals for your business and your company's performance. Those goals are definitely necessary and should be a part of your goal-setting practice. But don't forget about your personal life, too! Having a healthy mix of personal and professional goals is mutually beneficial. By working toward and meeting your professional goals, you'll be motivated to also continue working toward and meeting your personal goals, and vice versa. Momentum is momentum.

Setting goals is something I think everyone should be doing, whether or not you run a business. It's beneficial for many reasons. For example, if you're a new entrepreneur (or a veteran!), setting goals can be a great way to build your confidence. Especially as you track goals over time, you can look back and have a record of just how far you've come. It can also help you figure out a game plan. Because you are at the helm of the ship, so to speak, you might feel directionless or unsure of where to even

begin. Goal-setting can help with that, too, because you start with the big picture and work backward, breaking up a big goal into smaller, more manageable pieces. Goals can also be a great way to build healthy habits into your daily routine, setting yourself up for further success beyond just what goals you've set for yourself.

I have long loved goal setting. It is one of the best motivators for me. I set goals and work as hard as necessary to reach those goals, whatever they may be. However, I do want to caution against a pitfall I find myself in. I don't take enough time to celebrate, or even simply acknowledge, reaching my goals. I have a habit of setting a goal, and by the time I know I'm going to reach it, I've already moved on to what I want my next goal to be. By doing this, I rob myself of the joy of celebrating my wins. Do I need to throw myself a party with balloons and a cake? Certainly not. I do, however, enjoy taking a moment to reflect and feel proud of what I've accomplished before rushing off in pursuit of the next goal!

SMART Goals

A golden rule of setting goals is that they should be SMART. You may have seen this acronym before, but it really does encapsulate the best practice for setting goals. It's pretty straightforward and easy to follow. As you set your professional *and* personal goals, they should follow this framework:

 Specific: Your goals should all be specific and clear. The more details you can include to define what your goal is, the better. What do you want to accomplish, and why is the goal important and relevant to you?

 Measurable: Your goals should be quantifiable in some way. Instead of a broad-stroke goal that can be interpreted loosely, a measurable goal has a specific number or volume involved. For example, instead of saying that you want to "read more," a measurable goal would be that you want to "read 50 books."

 Achievable: While a huge part of goal setting is to push yourself to reach new milestones, the goals you choose should still be attainable. The key here is to figure out what will be a stretch without setting yourself up for complete failure. Consider the factors that might be potential roadblocks (financial, staffing concerns, time constraints, etc.).

 Relevant: If your goals aren't important to you or if they don't align with your values, you may as well not bother setting them because they will be so hard to stick to. Relevant goals are ones that have meaning for your personal and professional life. They are worthwhile and will deliver some kind of positive outcome specific to your priorities.

 Timely: Similar to the measurable point, goals should also have a specific timeline in which you want to achieve them. Expanding on the reading goal, just saying that you want to "read 50 books" isn't enough. Maybe you want to "read 50 books by December 31."

Brainstorm Goals

Use this section to start a brainstorm for one of your goals. Here you will identify what goal you want to achieve, build out the goal to make sure it fits into the SMART framework, and work backward to set your game plan for how to reach that goal.

PERSONAL / PROFESSIONAL (CIRCLE ONE)

SPECIFIC What do you want to accomplish? Why is this important to you?	
MEASURABLE How will you quantifiably measure your goal?	
ACHIEVABLE Is this a goal that will allow you to stretch while still being reasonable? How so?	
RELEVANT Is this a worthwhile goal to pursue? Does it align with your interests, values, etc.?	
TIMELY By when do you wish to achieve your goal?	

Write out your goal:

_____

_____

Break down the key steps you need to achieve, what each step entails, and the time frame within which each step needs to be completed.

KEY STEPS	DESCRIPTION	TIMELINE	COMPLETE
			☐
			☐
			☐
			☐
			☐

Sleep (The Key)

If I could give *one* piece of advice to new entrepreneurs or encourage them to do *one* thing, it would be to make sure they're getting enough sleep. Not getting enough sleep was something I used to do regularly, especially when I was just at the beginning of my career. And not only did I do it regularly, I prided myself on how little sleep I "needed."

SLEEP-DEPRIVED CARLY

Unfortunately, this lack of sleep was nothing to be proud of. Just because I was able to somewhat function the next day after a mere four hours of sleep, I needed more.

I wasn't staying up late and getting up extra early for fun. At the time, I was working a draining full-time job at a tech startup and then coming home to my apartment to work on my own website at night. Most nights, I wasn't able to close my laptop until well after 1 a.m., and my alarm went off around 5 a.m. every morning. I only caught up on sleep on Friday nights when I could sleep in the next morning. Then the grind would start all over again.

I did this in the name of hustle, and I wore this lack of sleep as a badge of honor, so much so that I would even post my sleep stats from an activity tracker I wore every day on social media. Just in case people didn't know how many hours I was working and how few hours I was sleeping, a quick screenshot of a four-hour night's sleep would do the trick. Looking back, I'm not only embarrassed that this was something

I promoted, but I also wish I could go back and have a do-over…and tell myself to get some sleep!

NEVER AT THE EXPENSE OF SLEEP

This is yet another trap entrepreneurs fall into. When there's a never-ending list of things to do, there's a pressure to feel like you have to cut out things—like sleep—to get it all done in one day, day after day. The reality is that you need sleep, and getting sleep should be celebrated because it will only make you a better leader. You will show up to work every day in a good mood with enough energy. You will be able to make hard decisions with a clear mind. The tasks you have on your list won't feel as daunting, and you'll even be able to get through them in a more efficient manner.

Sleep is key. Think of getting a full night's sleep *as a task* that you must accomplish every day for success. It's not simply something you should do; it's something you must do. It's not wasted hours.

Creating a Healthy Sleep Environment & Routine

Consider a night of sleep as something that is as important as staying on top of bookkeeping for your business. Part of getting a good night's sleep is setting yourself up for success. This involves creating a healthy sleep environment and a routine that facilitates great sleep. These strategies signal to your brain and body that it is time to unwind and time for sleep.

Start by describing your current routine and setup. You may want to do this while you get ready for bed one night. Take note of how you prepare for bed, what steps you follow, and how you feel throughout the routine.

_____

_____

_____

_____

_____

_____

HEALTHY SLEEP ENVIRONMENT CHECKLIST:

❏ Install black-out shades in bedroom.

❏ Charge your phone across the room, or in another room.

❏ Consider a sleep mask and/or earplugs.

❏ Remove the television (and other screens) from the room.

❏ Set up a sound machine.

❏ Bring in a fan or set the temperature a couple of degrees cooler at night.

HEALTHY SLEEP ROUTINE CHECKLIST:

❏ Set a desired bedtime by working backward from when you need to wake up.

❏ Stick to a "no screen" rule for 60 to 90 minutes before your bedtime.

❏ Find what helps you unwind: a breathing exercise, a warm bath, reading, light yoga, etc.

❏ Create a sleep trigger, like playing the same calming song every night before climbing into bed.

❏ Tweak the routine until it feels right...and then stick to it!

Sleep Tracker

As you work on your sleeping environment and tweak your routine, it can be very helpful to track your sleep in a log. This helps you understand what is working and what isn't. You may feel better when you sleep an hour *less* than what you thought. Or you may fall asleep more quickly when you take a bath before bed instead of reading.

	Mood Before Bed	Fell Asleep Quickly	Slept Through the Night	Bedtime	Wake Time	Total Hours	Easy to Wake Up	Mood Upon Waking	Energy Throughout the Day
Day 1		Y / N	Y / N				Y / N		
Day 2		Y / N	Y / N				Y / N		
Day 3		Y / N	Y / N				Y / N		
Day 4		Y / N	Y / N				Y / N		
Day 5		Y / N	Y / N				Y / N		
Day 6		Y / N	Y / N				Y / N		
Day 7		Y / N	Y / N				Y / N		
Day 8		Y / N	Y / N				Y / N		
Day 9		Y / N	Y / N				Y / N		
Day 10		Y / N	Y / N				Y / N		

Fueling Your Body

A common thing I hear and see with entrepreneurs is skipping out on eating and drinking proper meals and fuel because "there isn't enough time." I get it. I have been there myself. When the to-do list is a mile long and you have 20 minutes between meetings, you grab a power bar instead of sitting down for something more substantial. Then 3 p.m. rolls around and you still have hours ahead of you, but you're hitting the wall, so you grab your third coffee of the day to get through the afternoon slump. Then dinnertime rolls around and you're exhausted (possibly from work but also possibly from the lack of proper fuel…) so you order comfort food for takeout.

RUNNING ON FUMES

It's a cliché expression at this point, but your body is your temple. As an entrepreneur, when you're required to show up every day in your best shape to lead your company to success, you have to have the right fuel. Yes, you can get away with caffeine and sugar and simple power bars for a while, but not forever. At some point, these quick fixes take their toll.

Take it from me; I learned the hard way that I simply couldn't function long term without proper fuel. My vice was relying on caffeine, instead of food, for energy. At a certain point, my body called it quits. I ended up in the hospital and had a major, major wake-up call. I had this moment of clarity when I realized that I simply couldn't go on without putting my health above everything else.

THRIVING ON NOURISHMENT

Of course, I determined that I had to prioritize taking better care of myself. But I also realized that if I wasn't able to take care of myself physically, there was no way I could run a business. Sure, I was able to get through the day and I felt like I had energy (from all that coffee), but looking back, I realize I was more likely running on fumes. Unknowingly, I was sabotaging myself, and, by proxy, sabotaging my business, too. Now I know I had made poor decisions, felt increased stress over problems that shouldn't have phased me, and overall definitely held my business back. I confused any success as the max success I could have. Because I was able to make it somewhat work, I figured I wasn't causing myself or my business any harm.

With this in mind, I wonder how much further I could have taken my business and how much *more* success I could have seen had I been showing up every day as healthy as possible. If this kind of story sounds familiar, know it's not too late. Make the commitment to prioritize your overall health, starting with nutrition, to better yourself as a person and reap the benefits of being your best entrepreneur self, too.

Nutrition can be tricky though. Everybody—and every *body*—is going to have different nutritional needs. Understanding your own body and working alongside an expert like a dietitian can help you unlock your personal needs. The best part is realizing how proper fuel improves so many aspects of your life.

Fuel Diary

I'm purposefully calling this a fuel diary. This should not be a place where you judge yourself for what you eat or purposefully restrict yourself from certain foods. Instead, use it as a way to track how what you eat makes you feel. Proper fuel is key! As an entrepreneur with lots to do and not a lot of time to do it in, what you fuel your body with can make or break your day. Take note of what you eat and how your body reacts immediately after and over time as well. Be on the lookout for your energy levels and mood.

FUEL TRACKER

S M T W T F S   DATE:

	WHAT I ATE:	HOW I FELT:
BREAKFAST		
SNACK		
LUNCH		
SNACK		
DINNER		

Meal Plan

As you begin to better understand what fuels your body best (and what doesn't), it can be helpful to meal plan for the workweek. Even if you only plan out your breakfasts and lunches because they most impact your workday, this can ensure you always have the time to properly fuel yourself. Also, by planning ahead, you can avoid those panicked mornings when you're running out the door and just grab a coffee to drink instead of breakfast or lunches when you just have a power bar because it's the quickest thing on hand.

MEAL PLANNER & SHOPPING LIST

WEEK OF:

MONDAY
B: _____
S: _____
L: _____
S: _____
D: _____

TUESDAY
B: _____
S: _____
L: _____
S: _____
D: _____

WEDNESDAY
B: _____
S: _____
L: _____
S: _____
D: _____

THURSDAY
B: _____
S: _____
L: _____
S: _____
D: _____

FRIDAY
B: _____
S: _____
L: _____
S: _____
D: _____

SHOPPING LIST:

_____
_____
_____
_____
_____
_____
_____
_____
_____
_____
_____
_____
_____
_____
_____
_____
_____
_____
_____
_____
_____

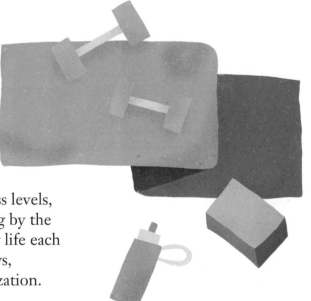

Movement

As your workload, and potentially your stress levels, increase, certain health priorities start falling by the wayside. Incorporating movement into your life each and every day can benefit you in myriad ways, but particularly as the leader of your organization.

IT'S ALWAYS A WIN

There's a good chance you already have some sort of exercise routine in place—in this case, great! Keep it up! (And keep it up especially when things get tough.) But if you haven't found a way to incorporate movement into your everyday life, now's the time to start prioritizing it. If you hate working out or breaking into a sweat, I hope I haven't lost you yet. There's a reason why I prefer labeling this as "movement" versus "exercise." Certainly, if you want to pound the pavement every morning to get in three miles before you head into the office, go for it. If playing an aggressive game of tennis on the weekend helps get out your frustration, go for it. If a virtual cycling class suits your fancy, go for it.

With that said, any kind of movement is beneficial. We are more and more glued to desks and computers. Even experts are coming out to say that "sitting is the new smoking." Your role as an entrepreneur likely has you logging extra hours in a chair. Whether you're leading meetings, answering emails, or communicating with clients, there are almost too many opportunities to sit.

I know whole days can go by for me when if I don't *make* time to stand up and move, I might not. The great news is that you're never wasting time by getting in movement every day. Remember, the theme here is that you have to be your best self to effectively lead your company. By prioritizing your well-being, you are prioritizing your company at the same time. And while you certainly are investing in yourself, there are plenty of ways this is also directly good for your business.

When you step away from your desk to get in some active movement, whether it's a full-blown workout or simply walking around the block, you give your brain a break from work. In this space, you can actively recover from stress and anxiety. During this time of movement, you can switch from active to passive learning and problem-solving. While it may seem like you've stepped away from work, and in a sense you have, your brain is still working in the background. Your next big idea could come to mind mid-downdog!

Easy Ways to Incorporate Movement

As I mentioned, you don't have to push yourself to extremes to reap the extra value of movement. If you absolutely despise working out, reframe it completely as "movement." You get the same benefits for your mental well-being (and business pursuits!), but it feels a lot more manageable.

- Invest in a standing desk, a tray for your stationary bike, or a treadmill desk.
- Walk or bike to and from work every day.
- Find a workout class that excites you to work out.
- Work with a personal trainer.
- Take work calls while you walk outside or on a treadmill.
- Instead of passive dinners or experiences, bring clients to fun workout classes.
- Wake up 20 minutes earlier to complete a stretching routine before you get ready for work.
- Take the stairs instead of the elevator on your way up to the office every trip.
- Suggest a walking meeting for one-on-ones with employees.
- Keep a yoga mat or light equipment in your office for when you have unexpected downtime.
- Get the whole team involved with group activities to encourage movement.
- Unwind from work with a workout.
- Hit a tennis ball back and forth with a friend.
- Give yourself different challenges to hit throughout the week or month.

Movement Planner & Tracker

The easiest way to make sure you have time for movement every day is to *create* the time for movement. Scheduling it into your calendar, with the same importance as a work meeting, ensures you always have the time. Everyone has different priorities and varying degrees of flexibility, so you'll have to figure out what works for you. You may create a standing "movement meeting" on your calendar every morning so everyone knows you won't be available, or you may look at each week individually and schedule it in when you know you'll need breaks.

MOVEMENT PLANNER

WEEK OF:

	MOVEMENT:	HOW I FELT:
MONDAY	_____ _____ _____ TOTAL TIME: _____	
TUESDAY	_____ _____ _____ TOTAL TIME: _____	
WEDNESDAY	_____ _____ _____ TOTAL TIME: _____	
THURSDAY	_____ _____ _____ TOTAL TIME: _____	
FRIDAY	_____ _____ _____ TOTAL TIME: _____	

ENTREPRENEUR:

AMBER FILLERUP CLARK

You have success with multiple companies right now—how do you think your working-out journey has helped you be a better entrepreneur?

For me, working out is honestly like therapy. I have done it consistently since I was a teenager. I feel so good after a workout that it just sets the tone for my day and gives me so much energy.

You work out pretty consistently while juggling work responsibilities and being a mom of three! How do you find time to fit it all in?

I usually wake up before the kids to work out. It was hard at first to get in the habit of this, but I love my mornings so much! I get to listen to music, get a good sweat, stretch, meditate, and think about what I have going on that day. If I don't feel like waking up early that morning, I will just work out with the kids. It's important to me that they see us being active, so often they will come join in and work out with me.

Business names: BFB HAIR and DAE HAIR

Business description: BFB is a hair extension company—we make extensions for the everyday girl! dae is a clean haircare company inspired by the desert! We have nourishing desert botanicals in all of our products and have a hydration focus.

How long have you been in business? BFB since 2016 and dae since 2020

Where are you headquartered? Arizona

How many employees do you have? Between both companies, we have 16 employees.

Do you incorporate any other kind of movement into your workday besides a traditional workout?

In the evenings, we play soccer with the kids in the backyard! Our son loves soccer. We ride bikes as a family at the park, swim in the backyard, or go hike in the desert. We try to be outside as much as possible.

What advice or encouragement do you have for a new entrepreneur who thinks there just isn't enough time in the day for movement?

If it's a priority, you'll find a way! My kids know when I'm working out that they have three options: (1) work out with me, (2) play alongside me, or (3) fend for themselves! It's only 45 minutes to an hour, and I welcome my kids being bored because that's when they end up going off and being most creative. The other part is, once you are truly consistent, eventually your body will crave it so much that it no longer feels like a chore.

Meditating

If you've ever met me in person, even for five minutes, you have likely heard me raving about how meditating every day changed my life. I know that it has become a clichéd thing to say, but meditating genuinely changed my life.

FIND YOUR CLARITY

When I visualize what meditating is, I picture a very specific thing. Usually someone sitting cross-legged on a floor, barefoot, hands resting on her knees. For years, I had heard the high praises of meditation. I just never thought it was "for me." Great for other people, sure, but not for me. This was solidified for me when a coworker and I tried to do a 30-day meditation challenge together at my first job. We both tried, and we both failed. Miserably. (Looking back, we failed because we had no idea what we were supposed to do.)

Fast-forward about half a decade, and I was persuaded to try it again. This time, instead of just diving in, I decided to use a popular meditation app. I watched all the training videos and committed to trying meditation for 30 days again. This time something magical happened for me. I understood what I was supposed to be doing—because I had done the research and followed the training (go figure)—and it clicked.

I had long thought that meditation was about silencing the thoughts in my brain. No wonder I found it impossible! It's not about turning off the thoughts you have, but instead learning to let them come and go freely, without passing any sort of judgment on the thoughts. The best way I've found to visualize this is to think of a blue sky. It's okay if clouds come and go; it's knowing that they will eventually pass and that even as they appear, the blue sky is always there.

Everyone can benefit from meditation, even small children. As an entrepreneur myself, I can tell you firsthand how useful the practice of meditation can be when you're running a company. There are high stakes involved here; you may have invested your life's savings into this company. There will likely be countless stressful moments when a team of people are going to turn to *you* for calm guidance. There is a delicate line you will walk to create a healthy work-life balance when building your dream company feels all-consuming. This is when practicing meditation can play a lead role in your daily life. It can help you build that muscle to find clarity during times of high stress and weather rocky times like a pro.

The ultimate goal is not to be perfect at meditating; it should be that you have this mindfulness skill in your back pocket so you can apply it throughout your day to stay calm and levelheaded.

Helpful Tips for Your Meditation Practice

You have probably heard someone mention that they have a "meditation practice" or that they "practice meditation every day." Using the word *practice* is not a mistake. You practice meditation because it's something you can always work on. There is no perfection here, which should alleviate some of the stress that may be associated with trying to meditate. Go ahead and take that pressure off yourself.

1. **DO A LITTLE BIT OF RESEARCH.** You do not need to get a degree from a university to understand the basics of meditation. There are plenty of resources out there that can give you the rundown of meditation. It's important to know what it is and what it is not.

2. **CARVE OUT TIME FOR YOUR MEDITATION PRACTICE.** Similar to creating time for lunch and movement, you should also carve out some time during your day for your meditation practice. While you can meditate for extended periods of time, start by trying to find just 10 minutes of your day you can dedicate to your practice. This may be sometime during your morning routine, at 10 a.m. between client meetings, or the end of the day before you head home. Especially at the beginning of your meditation journey, pick a time you know you can consistently stick to every day, and add it to your calendar.

3. **COMMIT TO A 30-DAY TRIAL PERIOD.** Don't feel like you need to sign up for a full-immersion meditation retreat right off the bat. Commit to practicing for 30 days in your everyday life.

4. **GET INTO POSITION.** It can be tempting to get nice and cozy to relax, but in the case of meditation, you want to be comfortable, but not too comfortable. Definitely avoid lying down or sinking into a big comfy couch. Try sitting on the floor with your back upright against a wall. You can use a small pillow or folded towel to sit on for a bit of cushioning.

5. **FIND A GUIDED PRACTICE YOU CAN LISTEN TO.** A guided practice, whether it's a free audio clip online or included in an app, can help you stay on track while meditating. Especially when you're just starting out, it can be helpful to have someone guiding you through each of your sessions. Think of it like having a personal trainer at the gym; you're doing the workouts, and he or she is just guiding you through what to do and when.

Mindfulness Practices

Even if you try this and it doesn't quite click for you, there are other ways to find mindfulness throughout your day. It's something you can practice at any point of the day to build up your meditation muscles. The more you practice, the more easily you'll be able to tap into this skill when things get tough.

BODY SCAN

This is a super simple mindfulness technique that you can do anywhere. It's great to do when you have three minutes at your desk alone, when you're in bed waiting for sleep to arrive, or even when you're sitting in the carpool line at your child's school. It's as simple as the name says: You scan your body, starting with your toes all the way up to the top of your head. As you move up your body, try to relax each body part, noting how each feels. Is there tension? A tingling sensation? Soreness? Just note the feeling, try to relax that body part, and continue on with your scan.

WALKING MEDITATION

If sitting still is especially hard, try a walking meditation instead. You can do this by walking back and forth in your office's hallway or while you're walking outside in nature. As you walk, take note of how your body feels with each step and what sensations you experience as you move.

5-5-5 BREATHING

Connecting to your breath is a simple and effective way to tap into a mindfulness practice. This is also a great option when you feel like you need to hit the "SOS" button, like if panic is setting in, if you're feeling angry, etc. Again, this can be done anywhere—standing up or sitting down! Place one hand on your chest and the other hand on your belly. As you breathe in, count to five at a nice pace. Then hold that breath as you count to five with the same cadence. Then release the breath as you count to five again. Repeat for a few minutes or until you feel a sense of calm again.

Journaling

It can be a polarizing subject. There are people who have religiously kept journals for years and years. And there are people (like myself) who have started and stopped as many journals as years they've been alive. There are also people who have never attempted. The reality is that journaling can come in many shapes and sizes. You don't need to open a notebook and kick it off with "Dear Diary" to journal successfully.

AN EASY OUTLET

I took an entrepreneurship class in college that really opened my eyes to the benefits of journaling while running your own company. Being an entrepreneur can often be an isolating position to be in, especially if you haven't found a welcoming community of fellow business owners yet. Friends and family may not understand the exact stresses you face on a daily basis. Not having a supervisor or boss above you can also be challenging. You might not have someone to help guide you through challenging times, to remind you to celebrate your wins, or to track and check in on your personal growth over time. Your journal can be a great place to help you process what you're going through in a judgment-free zone.

When you're in the weeds of running a business, it can be so easy to just get swept up into the day-to-day tasks without stopping to provide any kind of reflection points. Journaling can be the answer to this.

THERE ARE COUNTLESS BENEFITS TO JOURNALING. JOURNALING CAN:

- **Help you work through problems.** If you're feeling frustrated by an issue, try writing down what's going on. You don't need to go into problem-solving mode right away, but leave space to come back for brainstorming. A week from now you may find yourself with an idea, and you can quickly flip back to that page and add some additional notes.

- **Be a way to record progress over time.** As you journal everyday events, you are also essentially recording your progress over time. Progress is rarely linear, especially as an entrepreneur. If you're ever unclear of how far you've come or it feels like you've made no progress, you can flip back through your journal to see written proof—in your own words—of what your path has looked like!

- **Provide a judgment-free zone for venting.** When friends and family don't fully understand what you're going through, and when it's inappropriate to vent to employees, turn to your journal. Get everything you're feeling *out* of your head and onto the paper.

- **Guide you through challenging times.** One challenge I know I face while running my own company is that I wish I had a crystal ball or fairy godmother to just tell me what to do. When times get tough, you're usually on your own. Your journal can help boost your confidence to show you other challenging times you've overcome and help you work out your thoughts on paper.

- **Relieve stress, anxiety, and other negative emotions.** Writing down your thoughts and feelings in detail can help you process how you feel. Release any negativity (or at least help it loosen its grip on you) by transferring it to paper instead of letting it stew in your brain.

- **Allow a space for personal reflection.** Because you don't have a boss who can give you positive feedback about progress, try doing it for yourself in a journal. Praise small wins, commend progress, and celebrate success. Give yourself the pep talks and praise you deserve!

- **Inspire creativity and brainstorming.** Keeping a journal can also help you stir up new ideas and brainstorm through problems. Journaling might just give you your answer to your business's next big, great idea!

Creative, Low-Pressure Ways to Journal

Journaling is not a one-size-fits-all approach. If you're intimidated or turned off by the idea of writing in a journal, don't completely write it off just yet. There are plenty of ways you can reap all the positive benefits of journaling without committing to writing "Dear Diary" at the top of a composition notebook.

1. Write to a fictional friend.

2. Send emails to a separate email account specifically for journaling.

3. Download an app that serves as a digital diary.

4. Buy a planner that includes daily journal prompts.

5. Buy or create a gratitude journal.

6. Commit to writing just one sentence a day, every day.

7. Take photos and create a digital scrapbook by writing captions for the photos.

8. Sketch or doodle instead of writing.

9. Use your journal to collect quotes and thoughts you don't want to forget.

10. Collect mementos to stick in a notebook. Add a couple of thoughts for each.

Journaling Prompts for the Entrepreneur

If you need a little inspiration to feel comfortable writing, using prompts can help trigger your creative juices. Here are a few prompts you might find helpful on your entrepreneurship journey.

⭐ Talk about a meaningful exchange you had with a customer, and share how it made you feel in the moment.

⭐ Describe a challenge that you recently faced and how you eventually overcame it.

⭐ What are your top five proudest moments?

⭐ In your day-to-day job responsibilities, what brings you the most joy? What are your biggest pain points?

⭐ Is this the career you always dreamed about? In what ways is it similar to your dreams? In what ways is it different?

⭐ Share the best and worst moments of the day.

⭐ List five people who have been instrumental in helping you get to where you are today.

⭐ If you could go back in time and change a choice or decision you made related to starting your business, what would that be and why?

⭐ Explore any fears you feel may be holding you back from reaching your potential.

Relationships

Relationships can be complicated and messy and beautiful and wonderful. I would go so far as to say they are what gives meaning to the lives we live. Maintaining healthy relationships can be a challenge, even in the easiest of circumstances. When you're running a company though, you are going through a whirlwind of experiences and emotions that can spill over into your relationships. It can be tempting to pour yourself fully into your company, and often that's the impression people have. You see it in movies and read it in memoirs: the incredible entrepreneur who gave everything to his or her company, regardless of what that did to their personal relationships. (Sometimes building that company came at the expense of personal relationships.)

MAKE THEM #1

Here's the thing though: it's not worth losing your personal relationships, or even putting them on the back burner, to create a company. When you look back on your life, you will not think, *I wish I had spent more hours in the office.* You will think, *I wish I had one more day with my partner, my children, my friends.*

Maintaining healthy relationships while building a company is a challenge, but it's certainly not impossible, and no one is saying you have to be superwoman! It's a balance. There will be times when the business demands more from you and times when you need to give more to your relationships. It won't even be a clean 50-50 split. The key is that you have to continuously negotiate between your work life and your personal life.

There are all kinds of relationships, and, for better or for worse, they all require work and attention. It is worth putting in the work, early and often, because over time the relationship will strengthen. Healthy, well-established relationships that have been carefully tended to can weather storms. A friend who has felt your support over the years will understand when you need to pull away for a few weeks to handle a crisis at work. A child who has your trust will understand when you can't make a weekend baseball game. A romantic partner who knows you put them first when they need you most will understand when you need to dedicate time to your business.

Relationships are a two-way street, too. Your friends and family need you, but you need to lean on them as well. In the same way that carving out time for lunch to regroup and step away from work is important, it's just as important to spend time with the people you love! Spending quality time with your friends and family gives you perspective on what's important in life, provides you relief from work stress, and adds priceless value to your overall well-being.

Relationship Ideals

Prioritizing relationships takes work. It can help to start with a goal you have and work backward from there. This exercise can also help you define what healthy, ideal relationships look like to you. If at any time you find one of your relationships is not as strong as it once was, looking back at your relationship ideals can remind you what you're working toward.

With yourself: _____

_____

_____

_____

_____

_____

_____

With your family: _____

_____

_____

_____

_____

_____

_____

_____

With your romantic partner: _____

_____

_____

_____

_____

_____

_____

_____

_____

With your children: _____

_____

_____

_____

_____

_____

_____

_____

_____

With your employees: _____

_____

_____

_____

_____

_____

_____

With your friends: _____

_____

_____

_____

_____

_____

_____

Your "Non-Negotiables"

Finding balance between building your business and maintaining relationships can be difficult. There isn't a magic button to press that will solve the problems you will certainly face trying to fit it all in. Setting your "relationship non-negotiables" now is a great way to help your future self make tough decisions. When you have these written out, you can look back at what's important to you and what you absolutely don't want to miss. It can be simple things like wanting to be there to pick up your kids from school every afternoon or making sure that you have breakfast with your romantic partner every morning, no matter what. Record the events you certainly don't want to miss and what everyday moments you absolutely want to be there for so you can build your work life around these priorities.

With yourself: _____

_____

_____

_____

_____

_____

With your family: _____

_____

_____

_____

_____

_____

With your romantic partner: _____

_____

_____

_____

_____

_____

With your children: _____

_____

_____

_____

_____

_____

With your employees: _____

_____

_____

_____

_____

_____

With your friends: _____

_____

_____

_____

_____

_____

ENTREPRENEUR:

MARGUERITE ADZICK

Business name: ADDISON BAY

Business description: Addison Bay (AB) was born from the idea that activewear should go beyond the gym and where fashion forward doesn't mean less function. We make it easier to get dressed every day by offering the modern wardrobe for the modern woman. Designed for the girl on the go, produced by girls on the go.

How long have you been in business? 2018

Where are you headquartered? Center City Philadelphia, PA

How many employees do you have? 4 full-time, and 14 consultants and part-time

As a business owner, your time is a very limited resource. How do you make sure you give time to both your business and the personal relationships in your life?

The work-life balance is one of the hardest components to starting a business. My strategy from the very beginning was to be present—when I am in the office, I am fully present with my team, outsourcing all childcare responsibilities to our fabulous nanny. When I am home, I am fully present with my husband and kids, putting work to the side. I leave the office (almost) every day at 5 p.m. to relieve my nanny and give myself a hard stop. I definitely have to work at times once I get home, but I make sure to get in some solid time with my kids before signing back on.

As a female-founded and -led company, our marketing mission is to empower other women who are trying to juggle everything and do it well. I hope other women can understand and relate to my struggle of trying to "do it all"—this is not easy, and I'm trying to make it all work. Some days, I feel like I *can* do it all, and other days I feel like the worst mom and CEO in the world. As a female entrepreneur and mom, I believe in the importance of balance and know other women can relate to the same struggles.

Have you ever felt like you were letting down someone in your personal life because you were starting a business? How did you handle that?

Every day! The relationships that have fallen farther down on the list are my friendships. My family comes so far first, work comes second, and my friendships have unfortunately fallen a bit lower on my priority list. I have to pick and choose how I allocate my free time (a.k.a. time outside of the office), and 10/10 times, I am choosing to spend time with my kids. I say no to a lot of plans, lunches, and spa days, but I know I need as much time as possible with my kids to feel fulfilled, and that's self-care for me. The friends who get it are my everything—my tight group of ladies who are willing to come to my office for a coffee date or go to the playground with the kids as our hang-out time. They are the absolute greatest. My circle has definitely gotten a bit smaller in some ways, but it's part of building a business.

You started your company while pregnant with your first child. How do you think your role as "Mom" helped your business journey?

Being a mom has made my role as CEO a much more fulfilling one—work is very high on the priority list, but it is not my life. My kids bring such a well-rounded balance to my everyday life. It definitely makes for a very full plate, but I am fulfilled at home and fulfilled at work, which is the greatest feeling in the world.

My entrepreneurial and motherhood journey go hand in hand. I had the idea for AB for several years, but I didn't have the bandwidth to execute, as I was facing some serious fertility issues. At the time, having a baby was my first priority and I had to devote my time and energy to many fertility appointments. After several rounds of IVF, I was lucky enough to get pregnant with my daughter. I hit the 14-week mark and felt a sense of relief and had additional time to allocate toward something else other than fertility treatments. So why not focus my energy on a brand-new business?! I started writing a business plan and pitching the concept to investors, all while being pregnant with my first child. Having a baby and building a business at the same time, I kept getting the same question...are you insane? While it seemed absolutely crazy to start my own company while I was pregnant, it made sense for my life. I resigned from my job when I was six months pregnant

and moved into my office space/warehouse the next day to officially start AB. I launched AB when my daughter was 12 weeks old, and I haven't looked back since. My daughter, Annie, has been a huge part of this journey, from weekends in the warehouse shipping orders to visiting me at pop-up events. My hope is to inspire her to go for it, and the best way I can show her is to lead by example.

I was pregnant with my son, Behr, throughout most of 2020, and he played a special role in my life as a working mother. Like many other retailers, our day-to-day completely transformed. While I kept all of my employees hired full-time while they worked remotely for months, I went into the warehouse every single day to personally pick and pack all orders at ABHQ with my husband to keep the company alive—all while five months pregnant. At home, keeping up with a toddler and being pregnant were exhausting and amazing at the same time. That year not only impacted my business, but it also affected my life as a business owner and working mother. My little Behr was with me every single step of the year and made the lowest moments bearable.

What advice would you give an entrepreneur who has to balance all their relationships while starting or running a business?

Trust your gut, and set boundaries for yourself. Every day will be different. Some days will be more business focused and some days more relationship focused, and that's okay. The goal is to find a way to balance both at the end of the week, knowing you gave it your all at work and you were present for the people in your life. That's the best feeling in the world.

Mentorship

One unique relationship you shouldn't overlook is that of a mentor. A mentor is someone you can lean on to help with your professional growth. Mentors can come in all shapes and sizes, and each relationship is unique. You may have had a mentor at other jobs or at previous points of your career.

GAME-CHANGING ADVICE

In theory, it's a pretty basic idea. One person serves as the mentor and provides career advice and guidance, and the other person serves as the mentee and benefits from the guidance. In reality though, relationships between mentors and mentees can vary. Plus, it can be a tricky type of relationship to navigate. It's not exactly a friendship; it's definitely not like dating; and while the relationship is professional in nature, your mentor isn't your boss.

If you've had a mentor before, you know how invaluable they can be in your professional life. If you've never had a mentor before, there is no better time to find one than when starting (or running) a business. A mentor can be a game changer for you. Because you have no boss above you as an entrepreneur, they can help you work through problems, provide guidance on areas of business that aren't your strength, and overall provide support.

You might even find that the relationship is mutually beneficial for both mentor and mentee, where each receives guidance and support from the other to some degree. For example, you may be looking for a mentor who has significant prior experience running a business, and that person may very well learn from you about new practices, such as how to convert sales on social media.

Like any kind of relationship, you must build trust between you and your mentor. Because they are giving you so much (for free!), it's imperative that you show respect and gratitude for their help and support. Follow through on what you say you're going to do. Don't cancel at the last minute, and be prompt. Ask questions, but don't demand anything. Offer your assistance when possible. And don't forget to express your thanks for everything they do for you!

Finding the Right Mentor

If you're like me, you're probably thinking, *Well this sounds great, but how in the world does one find a mentor?!* Finding one who is a good fit can feel a little bit like dating: intimidating at times, awkward at others. You can take different approaches to finding one, from cold-emailing someone you admire to joining an organization that matches experienced entrepreneurs with new ones. Here is some guidance to help get you started on your search:

1 Know what kind of expertise you need the most or can benefit from the most. Are you looking for industry-specific guidance, or are you looking for general business advice that anyone who has successfully run a business can help with?

2 Know what kind of time and energy you are willing to dedicate to the relationship. Do you have the bandwidth for weekly meetings? Monthly? Do you need to meet locally in person, or is a virtual relationship something you'd be open to?

3 Make a list of people you know—don't just include potential mentors, but also people who might be able to assist in connecting you with a mentor.

4 Consider what you might be able to contribute to the relationship from your end.

5 When making your pitch, be as clear as possible about what you are looking for. Don't forget to say why you admire them.

6 Consider having an initial meeting before committing to a formal mentorship to make sure it's a good fit. If you don't want to continue, extend your gratitude for the time the person gave you. And if you do want to continue, be clear about how you'd like to set up more meetings if they are interested.

Mentoring Someone Else

An important thing to keep in mind is that as an entrepreneur, *you* may be someone a younger entrepreneur looks up to! Don't be surprised if an email pops up in your inbox with a request for coffee.

SOME CARDINAL RULES ABOUT PROVIDING MENTORSHIP:

1. Understand how much time you realistically have to dedicate to the relationship. Don't overextend yourself because you will be letting down both yourself and your mentee. If you can meet once a month, express that. But if you can only meet once a quarter, express that. If you don't have the time at all, politely decline.

2. Keep it professional and straightforward. Ensure that your relationship with your mentee is professional from the start and remains that way. It might be tempting to relax into something casual, but it's best for everyone if it remains professional.

3. Ask for the mentee's expectations before you begin. Try to understand exactly what they are looking for so you can make sure you are on the same page.

4. Provide guidance without telling them what to do. You want to guide, not instruct. It's okay if your mentee doesn't follow your advice to a T. This is a crucial part of their own journey, and it's okay if they do things slightly differently than you would.

5. Listen well and ask questions. One of the best things you can offer a mentee is a listening ear. It might be tempting to just want to jump in and help them by giving tons of advice right off the bat, but give your mentee the space to share their experiences, fears, and challenges. Don't forget to ask plenty of questions!

6. Celebrate their success! When your mentee has a professional win, be sure to celebrate it appropriately. This can also be a great time to offer them space for reflection on their growth over time.

Continued Education

When you start your own company, it can feel like a crash course of learning. Even before your business is off the ground, there is plenty to learn, and you very likely don't know everything you need to know right away. (Maybe you even feel overwhelmed about all the things you don't know yet just from reading this book.) Even if you do feel confident, there will be times when you simply won't know how to do something. If it were easy, everyone would do it, right?

LEARNING, ON YOUR TERMS

Because you feel like you're constantly learning, you may be inclined to think that it's enough. I would argue that it's actually more important than ever to continue to learn new things *outside* of your business. While it sounds counterintuitive, and you certainly have plenty of learning opportunities, finding ways to continue some degree of education outside of your business can make you a more well-rounded and grounded entrepreneur.

Do you need to enroll in a full master's program at a local university or sign up for an expensive tutor? No! That's one of the best parts about continued education outside of school. There are no rules and no constraints. You can do as little or as much as you want, without having to worry about being graded or how it will affect your future.

After so many years of high-pressure schooling, I was ready to never pick up a textbook or even learn something new. I felt like I had spent years learning, and frequently I was learning about things in which I had no interest. There wasn't a lot of joy in feeling forced into learning; it was a means to an end. (I will learn what I need to learn so I can get a good grade on the exam so I can get a good grade in the class so my GPA is strong so I can get a great job.)

Now that you are creating your own business, you can take off all those external pressures and start exploring the things you *enjoy*.

I realized how fulfilled I felt when I started to learn things on my own. After a trip to Paris, I was inspired to start learning some basic French. (I always chose more "practical" languages while in school.) One of my friends from high school taught a photography course, and because it was something that had always intimidated but interested me, I decided to sign up. Once when I was looking for a creative outlet, I dusted off my sewing machine and taught myself how to sew from videos online.

It's not always smooth sailing, and not everything relates to what I do on a day-to-day basis for work, but because I'm interested in what I'm learning, it's fun. Keep in mind that while the subject matter you're pursuing may not directly relate to your business, you are still constantly adding new tools to your tool belt that you can use in your entrepreneurial endeavors. You learn to problem solve in a low-risk environment. You may expand your network. You give yourself space away from your business, which can give you a new perspective that you can bring back to your company.

Finding Your Interests

So where to start? Without a course catalog and a list of requirements for your major, you may not know where to begin. You may not even know what you're interested in if your whole life you've been just checking boxes in the education department. Now is the time to explore what excites you and what you'd love to know more about. Consider some of the ways you might want to expand your skill set or knowledge:

What did you love as a kid? Did you dream of a specific kind of career? What obsessions did you have that you wish you could revisit and learn more about?

_____
_____
_____
_____

Have you ever watched a movie or read a book and couldn't stop thinking about the subject matter?

_____
_____
_____
_____

As you scroll through social media, is there anything you see someone else doing that you wish you could do?

_____
_____
_____
_____

If you had an extra hour every day to pursue a passion, what comes to mind?

_____
_____
_____
_____

Ideas for Continued Education

Don't be intimidated by "continued education." It sounds like a commitment, but it can be fun and lighthearted. Plus, there are so many ways you can learn. The best part is that you can do as much or as little as you want, and on your own time. It could be as simple as spending an hour on a Saturday morning working on a new sewing project or listening to audiobooks about the subject matter you want to know more about.

IDEAS TO PURSUE:

1. Research a particular period in history.

2. Take lessons to learn how to play a musical instrument, or pick up an old instrument you have long forgotten!

3. Challenge yourself to learn a new skill (such as photography, calligraphy, baking, etc.).

4. Ask a friend to teach you a hobby they love so you can do it together.

5. Take stock of skills you have but want to strengthen.

EASY WAYS TO LEARN:

1. Read books or listen to audiobooks on the topic.

2. Audit a class.

3. Find a course online to take.

4. Watch videos online.

5. Sign up for local lectures by experts in the field.

6. Hire a private tutor.

7. Visit museums.

8. Travel to new places, and immerse yourself in the culture and history.

Volunteering

As life becomes busy, it's easy to focus only on the things you have to do within your own household and office. It only gets worse as an entrepreneur. You will feel torn between your business and your relationships; when one thing gets crossed off your to-do list, two more items get added, and you probably spend a lot of your time away from the office still thinking about your business.

GET OUTSIDE YOURSELF

Volunteering can be a great way to step away from the stressors of your everyday life, both professional and personal. I know I fell in the camp of donating money to causes and feeling like that was the best I could do. But once I started to volunteer in person by giving my time, I felt a much bigger connection to the cause. I still donate money, too, but now I also give two hours of my time every week to a local food bank. Not only do I get to see the impact and necessity of the work firsthand, but I also have a greater sense of community.

Helping other people is the ultimate goal, but I also admit that it was such a game-changer personally and professionally. It felt good to be able to give back in a tangible way and provided a much needed perspective on what I faced work-wise. I found that volunteering made the problems at work seem much more manageable.

Finding a purpose outside of your work and personal life only adds more meaning to what you are able to contribute, and I think it's important to know that little efforts add up. You don't need to sell your belongings and uproot your family to give back somewhere halfway around the world as a full-time commitment. There are plenty of ways you can give back to your community, and you can still align the ways you volunteer with your personal interests and passions, or try something new outside of your wheelhouse.

Expand your impact by getting your whole team or family involved. It's a great bonding exercise, and you can maximize the amount of good you can do by bringing extra hands to the cause.

Finding the Right Organization

Once you decide you want to volunteer, your next step is to figure out *where* you want to volunteer. You can take various approaches, from seeking out causes that are close to your heart or matching your skills to what an organization needs.

Do you want to stay local or try something virtual?

What kind of skills are you able to offer?

What type of causes have touched your life personally?

How much time do you realistically have to give on a weekly or monthly basis?

Is there a local organization that aligns with your company's mission for team volunteering?

Have your friends or family had a good experience somewhere?

What organizations or causes have you previously donated to?

Skill-Based Volunteering

Volunteering your personal time is one of the most meaningful ways you can give back to your community. This is actually a pretty wide spectrum, though. You could volunteer an hour or two without needing any special skills, like how I volunteer at the food bank. However, this could be a great opportunity to use specific skill sets you already have. This is called *skill-based volunteering*. In addition to giving an organization your time and the specialized skills you already have, you can help the organization save significant money because hiring out certain skill sets can be cost prohibitive for organizations. It's a win–win for you and the organization.

1. Coach a youth league in a sport you used to play.

2. Provide free legal services to a local organization.

3. Mentor a high school student.

4. Give a lecture at a university on a topic you're an expert in.

5. Lend your hands-on skills (sewing, woodworking, etc.) to an organization.

6. Offer accounting or tax preparation.

7. Donate your graphic design talents, writing ability, etc., to a nonprofit organization.

8. Use your event-planning skills to help an organization run its next fundraiser.

9. Build an app or update a website for a nonprofit.

10. Shoot and edit photo or video content for an organization's social media.

Burnout

The whole point of the "Minded" section of this book is helping you avoid burnout, that is, a type of emotional and physical exhaustion from chronic work-related stress. You've likely experienced burnout at some point in your life, whether you were a student at the time or maybe working for another employer.

IT CAN HAPPEN TO ANYONE

I started my own business inadvertently during a period of burnout while in school. I was so emotionally exhausted and had all the classic symptoms of having burnt myself out from school work. I needed some kind of creative outlet that I could call my own and not have to worry about being graded on what I created. That creative outlet became my business over time, and my journey into mindfulness began after I experienced an extreme case of burnout. For years, I hadn't properly taken care of myself physically or emotionally. I had been getting by on fumes and shoving all my emotional issues into a proverbial closet until my body literally couldn't take it anymore. When my physical health collapsed, my emotional well-being went with it, too. This emergency situation inspired my pursuit of mindfulness.

Even if you've checked all the boxes and done all the right things, burnout can happen to anyone…especially when you're running a business. The work never stops, and the pressure can be a lot over time. Just think, even if there's just a slow drip of water, eventually a bucket will overflow.

If it gets bad enough, there will be no doubt in your mind that you're experiencing burnout. However, identifying the symptoms of burnout early can allow you to get on top of it and stop it before it gets too bad. There is a difference between feeling stressed every now and then (starting a business is not for the faint of heart!), but if it's an everyday occurrence that grows stronger over time, you may be at risk of burning out.

TELLTALE SIGNS OF BURNOUT

- Feeling dread about going in to work every morning or struggling to start new tasks
- Feeling pessimistic about your performance no matter what
- Feeling unhappy or even depressed
- Feeling physical symptoms of stress (racing heart, stomachaches, headaches, etc.)
- Feeling overwhelmed by tasks that previously wouldn't have phased you
- Feeling like you "can't take it anymore"

Stopping Burnout

So you've identified that you're experiencing burnout. Regardless of what degree of burnout you are feeling, you *can* get back in control. It will take work and some sacrifices, but it's absolutely possible to get back on track and back to feeling good about your work and positive about life.

1. **Seek immediate treatment.** If you feel severely physically or emotionally unwell, seek immediate treatment from a licensed professional. There is no shame in needing professional help. The important thing is that you recognize when you need it and seek treatment immediately.

2. **Tell a trusted person at work or someone in your personal life.** Often burnout can feel like a private event. If you're a leader within your company, you may have been putting on a brave face for everyone else. You may not have wanted to burden your friends and family with your stress. This is *not* a burden. Telling even one person you trust can lighten some of the emotional burden you feel, and that person can help you navigate out of burnout.

3. **Take note of what led here so you can look out for it in the future.** They don't need to be detailed notes, but just jotting down quick thoughts for your future self can help.

4. **Give yourself grace.** It is *okay* that you feel burnt out. It's really common as an entrepreneur, even when you "do all the right things." Don't beat yourself up over this. It's all part of the journey.

5. **Assess what's causing the most stress.** Try to identify what the biggest pain points are right now. Your biggest pain point may not be the most time-consuming work; it could just be the one thing giving you the biggest headache. Write down a list of your responsibilities, not in terms of what needs to get done, but instead in terms of what is contributing the most to burnout.

6. **Take things off your to-do list.** I know, you *own* this business. You can't just stop working. Instead, look for things you can take off your list right now to alleviate stress. Order takeout for a week. Skip cleaning the house for a week. (It'll survive.) Take some low-stakes items off your plate.

7. **Plan out your immediate next steps.** Getting to a point of burnout can be a sign of growing pains. It may be time to hire a new employee, or it may be a sign that what you're doing isn't working for your current life. Start by figuring out exactly what you need to do first and what you will probably have to do in the future.

8. **Press pause and step back.** When you're experiencing burnout, there's a tendency to feel like you're on a hamster wheel and you can't stop running. Give yourself permission to hit the "pause button" and step back from everything. You may need to step away for an afternoon, a few days, or a week. The world will keep turning. What's important is that you take care of yourself so you can show up as your best self.

Your Burnout Game Plan

You may have experienced burnout before, or you may not have yet. Either way, it can help to have a personalized burnout "game plan" ready to go in case it does happen. It doesn't have to be a perfect plan, and you will likely have to deviate in some ways and tweak it for each individual situation.

Who can I turn to at work when I'm feeling overwhelmed?

_____

_____

_____

_____

_____

_____

What person in my personal life can I lean on when I feel burnout coming?

_____

_____

_____

_____

_____

_____

What tasks can I let slip in my personal life if I experience burnout?

_____

_____

_____

_____

_____

_____

What are three things I can do outside of work immediately that will bring me relief?

_____

_____

_____

_____

_____

ENTREPRENEUR:

MIMI STRIPLIN

Have you ever experienced a period of burnout? Can you describe the experience and what got you back in the game?

We hear the term *burnout* so often, and many times I roll my eyes and think, *I'm fine—just need to make it to next Monday (or whatever day) and then I can take a break!* Typically when I'm facing burnout, I don't even realize it until it's a little too late. Burnout can look so different for everyone, and for me a period of burnout typically involves my daily rhythms being pushed aside to get just one more thing done (which spirals to 12 more things) quickly. My sleep schedule is off, eating habits ignored, and then one day I wake up and think, *How in the world did I stay alive through that day/week/ month?* I know, it sounds so dramatic, but I put so much energy into creating a life with healthy rhythms, and all of a sudden work takes over everything, which turns into burnout. Sometimes as a small business owner, it's tough to differentiate between being passionate or excited about a project and working yourself to no end and being faced with burnout. I think our society causes us to think that we must always be productive, but I'm so glad that I've come to peace with the fact that rest is productive for me. Being able to stay active every day, eat a balanced diet, get plenty of sleep, and just rest— whether that's spending time with friends or napping on my porch— are ways that I try to actively keep myself from reaching burnout.

Business name: THE TINY TASSEL

Business description: Brightly colored tassel jewelry, garments, and accessories, handmade in Charleston, SC. Recently opened our flagship store in downtown Charleston!

How long have you been in business? Since the summer of 2015

Where are you headquartered? Charleston, SC

How many employees do you have? 5

When I'm present and actively aware of my behaviors and habits, I am less likely to fall into a space of being burned out.

What strategies do you have in place to help prevent burning out?

It's taken almost six years to physically separate my workspace from my home, and I'm so grateful that this separation exists now—I didn't know how badly I needed this! I think for the first time in years, I just sit and watch TV without multitasking and making tassels or working on packaging products.

Do you have a specific person or set of people you can lean on when you're feeling burnt out?

My dad is always the first one to spot it! I never want to admit it when I'm in the thick of burnout, but I am so grateful to have my family and amazing team who are so supportive to encourage rest, healthy habits, and just time away (mentally and physically) from the shop.

If an entrepreneur felt themself burning out, what three things would you tell her to do right away?

For anyone who is nearing or facing burnout, just give yourself grace to stop everything you're doing. Add back in all 100 percent necessary things (like you will die without doing these kind of things...eating, sleeping), and then slowly add in tasks and work after truly seeing what is a priority and what can be delegated. I think most importantly, find time to truly rest. Commit to doing something every day for at least 30 minutes that you just genuinely enjoy!

Index

About the Author

A lifestyle blogger living in the tri-state area, Carly (Heitlinger) Riordan is the founder of Carly's Book Club, Carly's Stitch Club, and, of course, her eponymous blog CARLY (est. 2008). Carly is a "numbers person"—a graduate of Georgetown University's undergraduate business school, where she balanced being a high-achieving student, an athlete, and an emerging blogger. She turned her blog into a legitimate, successful business using the concepts she learned in school. She wholeheartedly believes any young woman should be empowered to flex her entrepreneurial muscle to merge great business sense with creativity and passion.

ACKNOWLEDGMENTS

This book would not have been possible without every single one of my blog readers, many of whom have been following along for over a decade! In a way, I feel like we have grown up together, and I have felt your incredible encouragement and support throughout the years.

I am also incredibly grateful for the support of my small virtual team for my business and this book. Specifically, Loredana Wulff and Raelyn Slaughter from Digital Brand Architects. I could not do what I do without you!! From DK, thank you Alexandra Andrzejewski and Jessica Lee for taking a chance on this book and bringing it to life so beautifully.

My friends and "coworkers" who provided vital moral support while I wrote this book during a super snowy winter, in a global pandemic, while pregnant...Ashley Chambers, Elsa Massey, Maddie Nassib, Kelly Larkin, Maxie McCoy, Melissa Smrekar, Nicole Driscoll, and Riley Sheehey—thank you for cheering me along!

For having my back and trusting me when I quit a job to turn my little blog into a business, thank you, Mom, Dad, and Stacy Heitlinger! I can't forget the whole Riordan fam for opening their arms and accepting me for exactly who I am.

Finally, I have the deepest gratitude to my husband, Michael Riordan. I truly could not have dreamt of a better partner for life. This was written during our first year of marriage and while we waited to bring our first child into the world. Thank you for the breakfasts in bed (all those English muffins!), for being a sounding board when I needed one and a listening ear when I just needed to vent, and for always believing in me when I wasn't quite sure I'd make it across the finish line.